On Borrowed Time

The Reinvention of a Lost Soul

A Self-Help Memoir

by

Anthony J. Williams, III

Thank you for taking this journey with me.

This started off as a way to heal. I have succeeded at that.

My hope is that, like so many other people, this book helps and moves you!

Praise for "On Borrowed Time
The Reinvention of a Lost Soul"

Almost 37 years ago when you were born, we could not be happier to find out that we had a son. After already having your two sisters, it was a welcomed and exciting time in our lives; our family was now complete. Three beautiful and healthy children; life is good.

As with every family, whether they admit it or not, there are always good times and bad. Some of those times are easy to get through and some are not. Our family definitely had a little mix of everything, but through it all we were always there for each other and always will be no matter what the circumstances.

We are so happy that all 3 of you have your own families now, so we can put to rest the fact that we always got accused by your sisters of loving your more lol. So, you can see how ridiculous that is because which one of your own kids do you love more than the other????? Hahaha

Anyway, I don't have to get into all that has happened because everyone who reads this book will find that out for themselves. For all the bad that happened we wish we could wave a magic wand and make that all disappear. For everything else, it has been a wild ride, and your dad and I are so very proud of the man husband, and father you have become.

Anybody that reads this book will see the strength and courage it took to get to where you are today. That and the love of your family which has never been stronger! To get handed all that life threw at you so far, and you always fought to get the upper hand, sometimes succeeding and other times not so much. But you always fought and that's all that counts.

If this book helps only one person, then that's one person no longer in pain. Your dad and I love you very much and always will, and we wish you only the best life has to offer from this point forward.

Mom & Dad

Introduction

Looking back over my life, the fact that I became a leader shouldn't come as a surprise to me. Similar to designing video games, the best results come from leading the player through a maze or labyrinth journey. In the game, you can create yourself to be anyone or anything you want, even a Super Hero!

I'm not a Super Hero, by any stretch of the imagination. All I have ever wanted is to be *normal*, if there even exists such a concept. Searching for my niche in life, I'm a husband, father, a young man in his prime, but I realize there are far too many heroes' journeys adrift in a violent current to support the reality of a *"normal human condition"*—one-size-fits-all!

When you're living "On Borrowed Time", there are no dreams, no future, no life. It's not like in the game, where there are do-overs, respawns, health packs, hints, and guidance. But in the game, I was able to be free, to be me ... to be just a regular guy or whatever I chose to create that day.

To say that my creativity saved me, is probably pretty accurate. I learned to fight and win against insurmountable odds and to withstand anguishing pain and defeat around every corner. I suffered health issues, injury, molestation, and addiction. But I also learned how to love. That's what really saved me.

I want to share with you my story in the hopes that some people out there who have given up, given in, been trodden down, merely surviving "On Borrowed

Time" will relate and can find the resilience to keep going, keep fighting, and believe in tomorrow. In the Game of Life, we can create a new reality every second of every day when there is hope, love, and belief in one's self.

It all has to do with the reinvention of a lost, confused, little boy and the games he played. The reinvention of my lost soul.

It all comes down to, "DON'T GIVE UP THE FIGHT!"

Anthony J. Williams III, Author

Testimonial for "On Borrowed Time"

A few months ago, I was asked by a good friend to critique and edit an autobiography of sorts. I set out to accomplish this task, and I feel that I let him down. During this time, I was dealing with some heavy personal issues, and instead of addressing and facing them head on, I chose to find solace at the bottom of a bottle.

As you'll see in the journey you are about to embark on alongside him, he knew all too well the dark corner I had hidden myself in. Thankfully with the help of family and Anthony Williams, I find myself in a much better place. But I digress. I chose to write this Testimonial and Review because regardless of time and distance, the man who has put these words to paper has always been and will always be more than a friend of mine; he is a brother.

High school was an awkward time for me. Leaving behind the structure and schedule of grammar school and entering a new building with new teachers and new rules and new people, the feeling of discomfort on the first day weighed heavily on my shoulders. I was introverted walking into Iona Prep, tucked away off a main road in New Rochelle, New York. On the first day of our freshman year, our homerooms were separated alphabetically. Had "W" not been so close to "Z," who knows if we would have become so close? He was sports; I was writing. He was the class clown; I was the quiet observer. He was the lady's man; I was the virgin. On paper, we were polar opposites, but through common classes and lunchbreaks, we quickly connected.

I credit Anthony with breaking me out of my shell. Senior year was a wild time for us. He would drive us home (I hadn't gotten a license yet), and we'd throw eggs out of his car at other students as they drove past us. We'd bring bats to school and go around the neighborhood and play mailbox baseball—I won't go into detail, but the statute of limitations must be passed by now—he taught me how to speak to women. We'd go to the movies and spot girls, me hoping to connect somehow from a distance, him determined to show me how it was really done.

We were wrestling fans. We learned the inside out of the business together. We practiced the moves on each other. Yelled at time and time again by our parents for roughhousing, we were just boys being boys. Until one day I power-bombed him on my sister's wood-frame bed; we were breaking things in Yonkers before ECW made breaking tables a wrestling staple. In the good times, he was my best friend. In the bad times, he was and is my brother. A man who was always there for me without question. A man who was willing to catch a flight from California to come to New York to slap some sense into me for becoming an addict. In reading the work you are about to read, I regret losing touch for many years.

Knowing the darkness that he has seen, I only wish I had the ability to turn back time in order to have been the rock and strength for him as he always was for me. He always inspired me, always pushed me, taught me more than he will ever know, and has always been one of my idols. And I say this including his faults. Why you ask? Because he faced them, he overcame them, and through the darkness he has built an absolutely beautiful family and a wonderful life for himself.

I am glad to call Anthony Williams a friend, but I will forever be honored to call him a brother. I rest assured that you, the reader, can find and be inspired by his story as I have been and still am. I leave this Testimonial and Review with a direct quote from my 1997 Iona Prep yearbook—and as Anthony knows, but you the reader may not yet, this quote explains four years of one of the best friendships the world has ever seen. A friendship that will continue to grow as we inspire support, and love one another unconditionally.

And with that, I welcome you to not only read, but experience "On Borrowed Time, The Reinvention of a Lost Soul" by Anthony J. Williams, III.

Keith Zuccarelli, high school and life-long friend

SECTION I

The Point of No Return

"What's a nice guy like me doing in a place like this?"

Chapter One: Revelation, *"What if there is no tomorrow?"*

New Year's Day 2004 was a bright sunny morning, cool breeze filling the crisp air. I was 21 years of age, a young man finally ready to face the world and call my own shots! It had been a long time coming for me. My early years were complicated by health problems and literally unspeakable trauma. This was going to be my year as 2004 ushered in a normal, adult life!

My eyes struggled to open as the first thought that passed through my head was, *"It must have been one hell of a New Year's Eve."* Yet somehow, I couldn't remember much, and something wasn't right when I pulled my hand out from under the pillow. The index finger on my left hand was about three times its average size. The color of my finger was just a shade shy of black. Confused, I tried to run through the jagged, sketchy scenes from the previous night to figure out how I'd hurt my finger, but the intense throbbing brought me back to the present. This wasn't normal, and I also knew this was not my doing.

I called upstairs to my mom and quickly walked up the steps to show her what I was talking about. Walking up the stairs only made the pain worse as my heartbeat sped up. The palpitating throb was so extreme that I considered using a sharp razor to cut my finger to drain the swelling and stop the escalating agony. I was still trying to convince myself that I'd banged my finger on something but just couldn't remember it.

My mother dialed the doctor's emergency helpline. My cardiologist called back, and Mom was instructed to get me to the hospital immediately. Cutting my finger to relieve the pounding pain was out of the question now because Dad had gotten involved. Within minutes, we were on our way to the hospital to meet with the cardiologist.

Panic began to set in when I was instantly admitted to the emergency room—not by me so much; this is what "normal" has been for me all my life, but rather for my parents. And rightfully so, they were grasping the reality long before I realized the severity of the situation.

All the tests conducted before this had never shown a trace of bacterial infection within my heart until today, January 1, 2004. It had just become a matter of life and death. This was the first time I had ever conceded to the fact that I had no control over the outcome. Laughter was the only way I knew to express my fear, so I laughed, reminiscent of the Joker's laugh from Batman. It sounded crazy and must have worried my parents because they asked me what was I doing?

We were told they would be administering a potent medicine that could cause hearing loss or the loss of my eyesight, but there were no other options at this point. Diagnosed with endocarditis, calls started going out to family informing them how dangerous this really was. This was the most scared I had ever been in my life. I couldn't fight or laugh my way out of this one. Now was the time to listen and take the advice of the doctors if I wanted another shot at life. I tried my best to digest what the doctor was saying, but this was a lot to handle on the day that was supposed to be the new beginning I had been waiting for my whole life!

I asked myself silently, not wanting to worry my parents even more, *"What if there is no tomorrow?"* As the gravity of the news sank in, accompanied by the excruciating insertion of a Picc-line directly into my heart for the drug that could save me or kill me, I began to wonder, *"How did I get here? So much has already happened to me! Do I even want to go on?"*

I felt battered and ripped apart by the needles and Picc-line (a direct line into the heart) and IVs; the blood pressure cuff was cutting off the circulation in my left arm; and all the while, I could hear the incessant beep of my irregular heartbeats through the EKG machine, like it was daring me to go on. Suddenly, there was only one question left, *"What if there IS a tomorrow?"*

Chapter Two: Survival, *"There was a whole lot more going on!"*

Right after the diagnosis, there were other confusing things happening all around me. Maybe this should have cued me in on the fact that I was heading strictly into "Survival" mode, but in my present state of mind—*yeah, a little hungover from the night before; okay, **a lot hungover**, and laughing like an idiot*—I may have missed some crucial clues along the way. Maybe even some hints from New Year's Eve while I made the rounds with friends. In the hospital, I was finally remembering that a few comments had been made that *"my skin color was off"* and *"I just didn't look right."* But who pays attention to that kind of chatter when you're drinking and partying? Everyone looks a little off, right? Well, no, not really.

I had stopped at my sister Tara's house to see family before I headed out for the evening, and remarks were passed back and forth expressing concern since my recent bloodwork, all routine with me, was not quite right. I chose to ignore all this, thinking nothing of it. Now, it was coming back to haunt me as I tried to just hold on. This setback could be cured or controlled like everything else I'd faced up to this point.

Tucked away in the corner of the ER with only my parents and a security guard, there was little else I could do but think about my past ... and my future. *Why a security guard?* I wondered. *Is this something extremely contagious, or did*

I do something wrong last night? Even illegal? Nothing was adding up. The security guard informed my dad that I could only have one visitor at a time. I thought it was really funny when Dad almost went through the roof with some emphatic, choice words. No one was going to keep my dad away from me at a time like this. The guard got defensive until the Doc came back and told him that my family members could stay with me.

Mom took care of the mountains of paperwork while I was transferred from an ER bed to a wheelchair to go to another room for the ordeal of inserting the pick-line. I just kept making jokes to get everyone else to laugh too. It was the only way I knew how to combat sheer terror and depression. My mind couldn't wrap itself around the idea that I could be dying. It did help to see the smiles on the staff's faces, so I kept up the jokes. It gave me strength.

I watched on the monitor as the Picc-line entered my body, holding my breath to offset the pain, and seeing the invasive black line travel all the way until it reached the interior of my heart. Wow! I felt like a test subject in a movie. And movies have happy endings! Or so I kept telling myself.

The next stop finally got through to me, though; that and seeing the look on my two sisters' faces when they rushed in to see me. They looked ghastly! What must I look like? I really wasn't feeling too great. My sisters had never looked a me like this before, except maybe when I was younger and fainted after leaving a doctor's office, smashing my face into the door. This, however, was much worse.

There was one more test to be done where a massive tube had to be shoved down my throat. I gave the nurses the fight of my life, and there was nothing my family could do but watch, be supportive, and pray. I lost this fight and when I finally started to cry, my cardiologist came over and rubbed my head. She told me she was going to do everything she could to fix me. With tears streaming down my face, unable to speak, I knew she read the message in my eyes, *"Help me!"*

This was when I started to pray.

Chapter Three: Truth, *"Nothing was ever going to be the same again."*

I guess you expect a week in the hospital to feel like a mini-vacation, everybody waiting on you and lots of attention. I couldn't have been more wrong!

There is nothing glamourous about being totally stuck in a hospital bed and having stinging needles poked in you every half-an-hour. It wears you out and dissolves your strength, so that even having visitors to break the monotony becomes exhausting, especially when you see the concerned looks on their faces. That drove it home to me more than anything else that this could be my last hurrah, my final battle.

This was also something new to me, like so many other events in my life have been, but this one could be permanent—I had to wonder, *"What happens to us when we die?"* I'd been so busy waiting for life to begin that I never thought about, *"What if it ends?"*

So many questions kept running through my mind. I realize now upon reflection that this silent, cerebral epiphany was what was wearing me down, wearing me out. I couldn't share these doubts and concerns. I didn't want to upset anyone. No one I knew, my age, had ever experienced anything like this. Who could answer all these questions? How would I ever get enough strength back to face the truth?

So, I pasted a smile on my face, which was rapidly waning, joked about having all the time in the world to draw, write, and watch TV, and I didn't have to compete with the other members of the family on what to watch. This was all my own show, and I was in charge! *"Yeh, right…"*

There were more and more questions as each day slowly ticked by. I knew my happy banter wasn't fooling anyone—everyone knew I was scared to death! *"Great pun on words, right?"*

We all knew in just one heartbeat, this could all go sideways. I had to keep up the façade of being the clown for everyone else's sake. The hospital was only the first step in the long, treatment journey. It would continue long past the hospital with no definite outlook or timeframe in which to heal.

The fact that there were no estimates of recovery time—no prognosis as the doctors say— led me to believe there was no hope. Yet, I kept up the act and pretended I was overjoyed when I was finally allowed to go home, only to be hooked up to another machine, just like the one I'd just left. Nothing really changed. In fact, in many ways it got worse because those sad smiles etched on the faces of my family were with me 24/7.

***

My mother, *God Bless Her,* took it upon herself to nurse me back to health with the assistance of at-home nurses. Sometimes during Mom's personal quest, I wondered whether it was a blessing or a curse, but now I'm convinced that I might not have made it without her.

I really don't know how she had the strength to put up with me with all my mood swings and anger and resentment … and the pain, the constant, crippling pain. Second to that, was the inactivity. The instructions were clear: There needed to be only the most minimal amount of movement for the duration of the treatment. And, you got it! From my perspective, there was no end in sight because no one could tell me how long this was going to last. No one would even hazard a guess.

The endocarditis, the infection, controlled me rather than us controlling the infection, but I did get to the point where I could withstand heart surgery when I became the youngest person to have a new, mechanical heart valve robotically replaced in my heart.

Yes, it was time to face the truth, the cold, hard facts, but I didn't want to do that! I still had some fight left in me, but in reality, *"Nothing has ever been the same again."*

It's now many years later and just last week, after I'd finished writing the first draft of this manuscript, I had my usual visit with my cardiologist. There is a very minor leak in my mechanical heart valve. What does this mean? Since my heart valve is not an end-all-be-all replacement for my original heart valve, there will always be and has always been a time limit on the valve. I have gone fifteen years with no problems, and right now it's not even an actual issue. It's a validation that my body knew something important was happening to me. I had been feeling anxious about it, but I chalked it up to the fact that I had just finished writing my story by basically reliving it all.

The good news is I am extremely healthy. These are the normal, *"par for the course"* worries that come with having a mechanical heart valve. I am in better shape than most and when you consider the amount of damage done to my body, it could be so much worse!

Now, I think I'm ready to tell you how I got here and *"What a nice guy like me is doing in a place like this."*

There's so much more to come. It's my hope that someone out there will gain strength from my story, finding someone in me who might be able to answer a question or two of the questions that only kept stacking up as time went on. I want whoever reads this to *"...**never, ever give up!**"*

Testimonial by Jodi

I met Anthony while I was in middle school. He was best friends with my best friend's brother. We spent a lot of time on 4th avenue in Pelham while growing up. Anthony was always kind and accepting to his friend's younger sister and friend (me). It wasn't until I was in high school where Anthony and I developed a friendship on our own. He would pick me up in his Cavalier, and we would drive around listening to music, usually Dr. Dread or the Halloween techno song, and laugh for hours. He would always listen to me about whatever drama was going on in my life and give me the best advice he could. I would often go to Anthony's hockey games to cheer him on. He was such an amazing player, and I was always in awe while watching him. Like most friendships, life happens, and we drifted apart physically but we have always had each other's backs up until and including today. As soon as I found out about his heart surgery, I immediately got into my truck and drove to Poughkeepsie to see him. I will never forget that day. Seeing someone who was always full of life and making everyone else laugh their asses off in the condition he was in, really took me back. It made me appreciate him and our friendship even more than I already had. 20-something years later and 3,000 miles apart, I still know to this day that I always have a friend in Anthony and that is something I will always cherish.

SECTION II

My Childhood

"When did it all start? You're not going to believe this one!"

Chapter Four: Reflection, *"Up until 2004, I still hoped for 'normal'."*

I began my story with the defining moment that altered my life for the rest of my days. Some people might say, I'm lucky to have days—*I hope months, years, decades*—ahead of me. I am now in my late thirties with a loving wife, two wonderfully healthy children, and a career I love, but I will never be "normal" with a mechanical valve stuck in my heart, ticking away the seconds of time until another option presents itself through the miracle of modern medical science… or not? It's a lot to have hanging over your head. I have to be cognizant of it and keep my general health and mental attitude in the best shape possible. What does this mean? It means I have to fight every day for the bounteous love and gift of life that I have been given.

In reflection, maybe all the other health issues, drama, trauma, and masquerading as normal that led up to my 21st year were merely dry-runs preparing me for this part of the journey, which didn't stop after the heart surgery. Oh no, I still had to make my stupid mistakes like everybody else and around every corner, there always seemed to be another hurtle to clear that I just couldn't quite get over, but somehow just skimmed across. So, I'm a fighter, a jokester, a philosopher of life, but really just a regular guy who has to keep picking himself back up and marching forward into the great unknown. *Just like everybody else…*

The journey we are about to embark upon has required strength, resolve determination, failure—*Oh, so many failures!*—and success. This is my life, my normal, and I welcome you to it in the hopes of aiding others who have to face and withstand what they perceive as insurmountable obstacles. Before I dive in and take you with me into the deep end of this pool of challenges, I must say without my parents, sisters, all my family, I never would have made it!

***

I was born into a "normal" suburban family in New Rochelle, New York, a mere 20-minute drive from Manhattan. I have two older sisters, Michelle and Tara. My parents are saints in their devotion to all three of us, but they certainly didn't sign up for the fear and turmoil that I would bring into their idyllic family dynamic. And when did it start? Yeah, I said you weren't going to believe this one—right after I came home from the hospital.

My parents and sisters were thrilled with my addition to their perfect dream of the future. I made the family complete. My folks had two beautiful daughters and a healthy baby boy. There was no reason to think otherwise. The doctors had given both my mother and me a clean bill of health before we were released from the hospital.

We're a close-knit family and that's been my saving grace. We would need to be in order to overcome all the trials and tribulations that I would introduce into our household. I want to state at this point in the journey, the beginning, that this story would never have seen the light of day without the support and blessings of my entire family. They've been pulling for me since the first day I couldn't keep any food down as a newborn, and they continue to do so to this very day. And I've really put them through a lot!

The throwing up of everything that passed my tiny lips stretched into weeks. My mom thought it must be *colic*. All babies have a little of that, right? Well, when it gets to the point that the baby isn't keeping any nutrition down and starts dropping rather than gaining weight, it's a problem. My life, from the beginning, would come with contingencies that would cause the entire family, but especially myself and my parents before I was old enough to make my own choices, to be riddled with quality of life decisions every day, every year, every moment that I drew breath.

There was no warning or explanation when I started throwing up everything I ingested. Thankfully, it didn't become a life or death scenario because I was diagnosed and treated immediately for Pediatric Hypertropic Pyloric Stenosis. What is that? Well, most people have never heard of it. It's so rare that there are less than 1.5-4 cases of it per 1000 newborns in the United States among Caucasian births and even less for African American and Asian American infants. The Pylorus valve from the stomach to the intestine is too narrow, thus causing a Gastric outlet obstruction. There are instances where babies grow and the valve expands, so time is the healer. In my case, that didn't happen. I required surgery at six weeks old to enlarge the Pylorus valve.

My parents have talked to me a little bit about their fears when their tiny six-week old baby went into surgery. It must have been hell for them. And what did they tell my sisters, who were so young yet excited to have a baby in the house? It couldn't have been easy. There were so many things that could have gone wrong on such a small, now undernourished, infant. But I came through it with flying colors. Everyone thought my problems were over, and I was back to being a normal, healthy, thriving newborn.

Well, that didn't turn out to be the case either when a heart murmur was detected, out of the blue, at two years of age. I'm not a doctor, and what I know about medicine has come only from my own experiences, but is there a correlation between a defect in a stomach/intestinal valve and the problem with the mitral valve in my heart? No one knows, not even the doctors, because these conditions don't really fall into the hereditary or birth defect category. They're known as congenital defects that just happen for no reason. *"Why me? Right?"* No, not really, I was also given the strength and fortitude to fight this, and there's so much more to come!

So, hold onto your hats, and let's laugh our way through the roller coaster ride of tears and fears that was my childhood. As I said, "You're not going to believe …" Yet, throughout my childhood and teens, I still believed *"…normal was possible.*" And that's all I've ever wanted. I will repeat, my life is now as normal as it gets … for me.

Chapter Five: Speculation, *"So what were my parents going through?"*

An active, inquisitive two-year old—the terrible two's, right?—*"How ya'gonna' explain a heart murmur to a headstrong toddler who wants to get into everything?"* Well, that probably didn't happen; couldn't happen. So, you try to stand back, let them fall, pick them up, kiss their boo-boos, and let them keep on running. As a father myself now, I worry about my own kids just meandering through the house without scraping a knee or bouncing their noggans off the floor, and they're perfectly healthy, yet headstrong, like me. And the worries never stop, do they? No matter what age they happen to be. Mom and Dad have demonstrated this so admirably to me.

It must have been a constant struggle for my parents, but mostly my mom. She was home all day with me, as her youngest child. The girls went to kindergarten and grade school; Dad worked all day as fathers did back then. As I mentioned, we were a normal, suburban family.

After school, kids would be outside playing all the time, and even at pre-school age, I didn't want to be excluded; nor did my sisters want to exclude me. I didn't yet know what "normal" meant, but I was already reaching for that ultimate plateau. I just didn't know what it was called at the time. My mother must have een shaking in her shoes every time she allowed me out of her sight. *How did she* *o it?* I mean, she had things to do too, like keeping us all fed, bathed, loved, and he house in one piece with three screaming, playful children just wanting to be kids!

I remember all through my childhood that Dad worked his tail off for long hours with barely any sleep, so he could provide for all of us. He did a great job because we never missed a meal. He would come home and try to give Mom a break from mostly me, but Michelle and Tara as well. Mom was amazing at juggling three kids, cooking, cleaning, and handling all the shopping. No wonder Dad never got any sleep with keeping his eyes peeled on me every evening, so Mom could get a few hours of respite. What did this worry and concern do to their marriage? I guess it just made them closer because their marriage is still the ideal that I strive for in my own.

When I was old enough to think about my health and what a heart murmur really meant—because my parents never kept anything from me—I was positive that it was caused by a dreadful hereditary condition, something tainted in my blood that made me weak and different. In fact, I believed this for the majority of my life. I wouldn't find out until my later years that it's actually caused by having rheumatic fever or strep throat at a young age. It wasn't until my twenties that I found out it was not a birth defect, and what a relief it was to me, but I still had to deal with the repercussions of this, especially after endocarditis changed my past and future in single blow, just as I was entering manhood.

The murmur during my formative years meant an extra doctor visit every year, antibiotics before any dental work even a routine checkup or cleaning, and special clearances from my physician to play any sports. To say that I felt branded would not be an understatement. I was very drawn to sports from cousins and family that were all older than I was, so there was no option but to play against the bigger kids. As the youngest, I had to earn their respect and that's exactly what I intended to do.

Growing up is tough on all kids. You're always looking for your own way and what sets you apart from all the other children around you and family members too. Adding a heart condition into the mix, meaning I couldn't play sports with my classmates, was a huge disappointment, especially since I wanted it so badly. Unfortunately, kids can be so cruel when they're searching for their own identity. Maybe they don't always mean to be, yet some of them do it on purpose to make themselves look cool and superior. You get labeled instantly and easily in school: weak, different, sissy, sickie, whatever? Yet, I was lucky in my early school years for I was accepted pretty well since I learned to be the class clown to make everyone laugh with me. You could always count on good ole' Anthony to come up with the most original and funny jokes. This creativity and coping effect followed me into adulthood. So, thank God, He blessed me with a quick tongue and a sharp mind.

It wouldn't be until I was a little older that I would face devastating challenges due to not being able to play sports. Even from a young age, I didn't take it lightly when I was told I couldn't do something. I was willing to fight for all it was worth to have a normal, competitive life.

And all the while, my parents had to sit by and watch this happen to me, knowing it was eating me up on the inside, even as I told jokes and laughed my tears away. I realize now that they have always been able to tune into my creative comedian personality. I'm sure my mother cried in secret and my dad shook his head in helplessness as they watched me blunder and bubble my way through school, always wanting something I could never have.

This is my own take on *"what my parents must have been going through at this stage of my life."* Believe me, it only goes downhill from here with, thankfully, a few highlights of success. We must all reach for and cherish those golden moments of *"making it"* because they can be few and far between.

Chapter Six: Dreams, *"Yeah, I had a dream that wouldn' let me go!"*

The thing about "dreams" and making them come true by achieving a major life goal that you can take pride in, is thoroughly knowing the dream inside-out from the *git-go!* You have to define and vocalize, even if it's only softly to yourself—what it is you want; the steps it will take to accomplish the goal; and establish a timeframe with a "Game Start" and "Finish-line" in place. Sure, this is like a rough draft, of course, and you must be malleable enough to recognize when it's time to make a change. In my case, *kicking and screaming every step of the way.*

It's interesting to me now that I'm older to realize that I was conceptualizing like this as a little kid. I'm talking about as young as 8 years old. It may sound strange to some people, but this is just the way my mind works. In the Introduction I said, *"In the Game, you can create anyone you want to be; even a Super Hero!"* I think I adopted this method of visualizing goals and dreams because I felt I had to give myself *'a step up the ladder'* because of the restrictions placed upon me due to the heart condition. *"Oh yeah, there was no question in my young mind that I had been cheated, especially in regard to sports!"*

So, my biggest dream, even bigger than *'having a normal childhood'*, was centered around sports. I was so sure that I was going to prove to everyone that I was made of sterner stuff than what was supposed to be *"normal"* for a kid with a heart murmur. After all, I was *"...the Super Hero!"* And even though I grew up in the decades when kids' video games were already all the rage, I wanted to be more physical, so I really wasn't that interested in them. *"Go figure..."*

When I was just 8 years old, I had my dream mapped out and ready to go! All I had to do is get the doctors' and my parents' approval. The rest of the story would write itself, just as I had laid it all out. *"Pretty strange for a second/third-grader, but since this was also my coping mechanism, firmly entrenched, maybe not all that weird."*

It all comes down to your comfort level. Seriously! Today, we automatically on a subconscious level guard ourselves against being too open-minded, too honest, too vulnerable. These are learned responses; whereas as a child there is more freedom to just feel good, to tell the truth, to love and be loved unconditionally. Everything should be about love, play, and fun. That's the type o early childhood I had and what I wish for my own children, as well as all the othe children of the world. This is the stuff Super Heroes are made of, and I was n exception to this normal progression of dreams. I was full of energy and that alon could wear some people down—*"My poor parents..."*—but I would always leav kids and grownups alike smiling. That was as natural to me as seeing and believing in my dreams.

I learned to skate with my whole family at an early age. I mean, it was New York with long winters and no shortage of ice. With skating came competition, hockey! At 8 years old, I decided I was going to be a professional hockey player for the incredible New York Rangers!

It took two full, agonizing years of waiting, but right before I turned 9 years old, one of my dreams came true. I remember it like it was yesterday. The heart doctor who had already turned me down twice completed all the testing and exams that were normally done and left the room, asking my Mom to step outside. *"It didn't look too promising at that moment."* But when they both came back in the exam room, there were big smiles on their faces, and I just knew. *"Yes! Step One of my dream was won/done!"*

I wish I could end this chapter entitled "Dreams" on such a positive note, but I can't. I wouldn't be honest if I didn't tell you now, right up front, that something else was going on that changed me from the happy-go-lucky little boy I've been describing to you to someone distrustful, confused, secretive, and victimized. You couldn't tell it on my face. The smile and jokes were still as ready and hilarious as ever, maybe even more-so, but now it was a mask I hid behind. This traumatic, life-altering series of events started when I around 8 years old.

So how did it all go wrong? How could a confident, energetic little boy just become miserable and locked inside his own mind, his own prison? *"Why didn't I say anything? Why didn't I fight back with my big plan and all my dreams set in place?"*

There are no answers, just unusual questions for a young kid to be asking himself when he's just joined the "Game of Life" as a Super Hero.

SECTION III

Hockey!

"Hockey was my life, my passion, my goal as a

Super Hero!"

Chapter Seven: The Game, *"I was going to make hockey my life!"*

Two polar opposites were raging a battle within me as I threw myself into hockey. Suddenly, making the team was all that occupied my mind, time, and effort. What a shame it would be if I'd waited all this time for my dream to come true, then I didn't rise up and conquer the challenge. I kept the traumatic events that were also a part of my life tucked away somewhere deep within me. It wasn't a burden as long as I had hockey to concentrate on, train for, live for. It was my passion, my focus, and my salvation during those grade-school years.

In reflection, I don't know if this was good for me or just covering up emotions that would come to haunt me later in life. Emotions that have never left me to this day but have continued to fester just beneath the surface of my consciousness. The time must come in everyone's life when you have to face your fears. Fear motivates us, but it can also be the most toxic asset we carry. The only way to control your fear is to accept and respect its power.

As an 8- to 10-year old, I wasn't equipped to handle these conflicting highs and lows. I'm sure the values and unconditional love I accepted and expected from my parents and sisters were jeopardized, but if I didn't "point the finger" or "play the victim" maybe I could pretend it wasn't really happening. Now, I can only tell my story the way I lived it. If I was confused over the events I couldn't control in my life, it was all part of the growing experience, and I was *only* grooming myself for a lifetime of hockey. I had the drive to keep my mind busy, concentrating on my dream and letting other issues stew in their own juices. ***"Hockey literally became LIFE!"***

***

I certainly wasn't the biggest kid on the block, in school, and especially in my extended family which included cousins, aunts, uncles, etc. So, in my formative years, I found myself playing hockey with kids bigger and stronger than I was. Ya'know, the "normal" kids? Always my health issues would cast a shadow over me wherever I went and whatever I did. Maybe I could hide from the other uncomfortable incidents, but I couldn't hide from what was common knowledge to everyone around me. Yet, I played hockey without fear, throwing my whole self into it. I didn't care how big, how strong, how good at the game the other kids were, I was going to show everyone that I could score goals!

Throughout my childhood—actually for my entire life, even today—it didn't matter the sport or the cause I was aiming for, my family was always supportive of me and my decisions. I don't know whether they agreed with everything I attempted or not. That wasn't the issue. They never argued or tried to sway me away from what my stubborn mind had zeroed in on.

Their support and encouragement would become even more crucial the older I got as the decisions kept getting harder and more difficult to manage. These are the types of decisions that many normal kids never had to face or if they did, they never recovered from it when something went wrong, or some people just give up without really trying.

"Can you see why I'm so motivated to tell my story? Life doesn't have to be this way!" We just weren't the type of family to ever give up on anything, and none of us are shy about saying what needs to be said. We pushed with all we had in unity to achieve more and become better people, but never to the breaking point.

Both of my older sisters would stick up for me when bullying and ridicule reared its ugly head. They refused to tolerate it. Even if they weren't happy with me because of something aggravating I'd done to them, which happened a lot with my headstrong nature, they put their personal problems aside and handled what had to be done. Yeah, they went back to being irritated with me afterward, but I knew they loved me, as I love them. If I never said it before or never said it enough times *"Thanks, Michelle and Tara. Thanks, Mom and Dad. I love you guys!"*

Since I was the youngest, by the time I was of an age to be on equal footing with the family, my sisters were grown and graduating from college, but we went to the same elementary and middle school for a brief period. Holy Name of Jesus in New Rochelle, New York, was where I attended elementary and middle school

Just a year ago the original building was closed when Westchester County voted to move the school. I remember a nostalgic feeling of remorse because I had made many friendships at that school, but like so many other people, friendships in early childhood just vanished with time. Yet, this is important to me because this was where hockey became my heart's desire, and I know anyone who remembers me from those early competitive years will identify with me through my love of the game, hockey.

TESTIMONIAL BY ALEX GIANELLA

Anthony and I went to school together as kids at a small Catholic school in NY; he was a bit younger, and I was friends with his older sister. A neighbor of mine was a great hockey player, and I remember seeing him and Anthony taking slapshots against the garage as a little kid. We had a park near our house where an old school had been torn down and all that was left was the concrete slab upon a hill. If you ever needed to find the hockey players, you could go by there pretty much any time of the day and you'd see Anthony and them playing street hockey on their roller blades. His success in hockey years later never surprised me; you could just tell he loved the game. I remember hearing he had a heart condition when I was in 7th or 8th grade and I was so confused--I never saw Anthony not smiling; he was an athlete and seemed happy all the time. I remember thinking how cool it was that he carried himself like that even though he was going through stuff. We lost touch for nearly 20 years, then reconnected on social media, and I was glad to see he hadn't changed. Anthony was happy and living life to the fullest!

Chapter Eight: Preparation, *"I had already been prepping for years."*

Long before I got the cardiologist's approval to try out for the hockey team, was living the dream and going through rigorous, self-imposed training so I'd be eady. All I did every day, every hour, every moment was play hockey and practice hockey at home, in the street, in the park, at the rink with my friends at school and in the neighborhood whenever and wherever I could.

When I wasn't playing or practicing, I was thinking about my next chance to play and developing strategies in my mind that I would later try out against bigger kids, older kids, and even when I was working on the game by myself. I didn't need anyone to play against. Sometimes it was just me, an imagined or jerry-rigged puck when I didn't have the real thing, an improvised stick or none at all, and any surface could be augmented in my inner vision to have the unpredictability of slick, silvery, shining yet treacherous ice.

Let's face it, in the late 80s and living in New York State, summer or winter, spring or fall, all the kids in the neighborhood were hooked on hockey. The Rangers were a hot team! Still are, for that matter, and it was a way of life for all of us, but I took it so much further than anyone else because I had more to overcome and more to prove.

"This is how you make your dreams come true—stubborn determination. Yeah, I'm sure I was really annoying at times, but I'm not embarrassed to admit that I was totally obsessed with the sport. I had waited so long, it seemed, to find my niche!"

I spent hours and days and weeks in the basement of our modest suburban home, making it my personal mini-rink to practice shooting pucks day and night when I couldn't find anyone else to play hockey against. In my rink, there were always plenty of roaring spectators and imagined hostile goalies to best with each puck I sent sailing into the netted goalmouth. My parents did get a little irritated with me when the basic white washer and dryer became slashed with black rubber marks that would never come out. Somehow, someway, I found a way to play hockey 24/7; I even dreamed about it in my sleep.

Me and some of my friends developed the game of "Sock Hockey" for when we couldn't be outside. We'd roll up a couple of socks to use as pucks and our hands were the sticks. The whole gang of us could be quite creative in a pinch.

Having your life's ambition tailored to perfection at barely seven years old and suffering through two denials for two extremely long years, never daunted me in the least. I just kept playing, kept shooting goals, and *kept at it!*

***

During the time when I was nine and ten years old, things began to change for me mentally and physically. I experienced my biggest accomplishments but suffered with my most burning secret. I would think that I had carefully hidden it so far within me that it wouldn't surface even for me to dwell upon, but it would always rise to the top of my consciousness when I was alone or in the dark of night.

Practicing hockey was how I rid myself of the demons and the confusion. *"Was this unwanted attention my fault? Had I somehow caused this to happen to me by something I did or said?"* So, on many nights, I'd give up on sleep and sneak down to the basement or imagine skimming over the ice in my small bedroom thumping whatever item I had picked up against the soft pillows of the bed, reaching for the high shots above the goalie's gloves, but below the net.

***

I made the cut the first year I tried out after the doc's go-ahead! It was my greatest achievement, but also the toughest year for me playing hockey on a team. Since I had been prepping for so long in small areas or the great outdoors, more without skates than with them, I couldn't stop on the ice and just plowed into the boards, but my coaches assured me that I put my whole heart into the game.

That first year was the most I was ever critiqued, criticized, and belittled by other players, both on my team and the teams we played against, but I had worked too hard for this and I wasn't going to let what other people said turn me against my dream. I knew I wasn't really that good at hockey when stacked up against the competition, but I had earned the right to be there.

My parents and other members of the team helped so much by taking me to Hommocks Ice Rink in Mamaroneck, New York, almost every weekend where they allowed me to slam into the boards until I learned how to stop. It's something no one can really teach you. You just have to figure it out for yourself—momentum and speed and constantly changing conditions on the ice. Every year as you're growing up this is different too as you change height and weight and coordination. *Can you imagine how hard that must have been for my folks? Especially for my mom?*

It was amazing that I never seriously injured myself or broke any bones in those clumsy, awkward training sessions. I know my family must have been feeling every crash against the boards right along with me every time they adverted their eyes and heard the deep, dull *"thunk!"* that was my helmet or my face and head if my top had popped off, my shoulder or hip, or the rough scratch of the thick, heavy blades. I know in this day and age in a public rink, you're not allowed to topple into the boards, as if on purpose, and it probably wasn't even allowed way back then, but I did it anyway. This was just another step in my life's ultimate goal, my dream, and finally sore, battered, thick-headed and all, I got it together and learned how to stop. I laughed like a silly clown with my face covered in bruises and a big toothy

smirk that said, *"I'm going to grin and bear it 'til I do this or knock myself out!"*

"If the years of prep didn't kill me, the rest was going to be easy-peasy. I

had made it!"

Chapter Nine: Childhood, *"I guess it's time to talk about the secret."*

There are many reasons why someone would want to relive their childhood. I'm sure with what you've learned about me so far, it's no surprise that I would like some *"do-overs"; wouldn't we all?"*

Reflecting on what made us the adults we have become, however, brings balance and, hopefully, closure for the things we cannot change and understanding for the decisions we made. Yes, hindsight is definitely more accurate than forethought, but a blend of the two opens up the path on our journey to healing, acceptance, and the ability to move forward instead of becoming stagnant. I was stagnated in many parts of my life for a long time. I had to work through this. This book is my final preparation for the great unknown ahead of me. I hope it helps you as well to relive, experience, cry a little bit, and not be afraid to look back on secrets and the repercussions.

***

As hockey became the most important thing in my life, there was a huge shift in my youthful psyche. I had proven to myself that I could do something that wasn't expected of me. At nine years old, I thought everything would be as smooth as untouched ice from here on out. *"Ah, yes, the dreams of the young. I hope I never* top dreaming at any age! We must teach our children to dream too. If you don't have a dream, you don't have a plan!"

In my case, my innocence was drained instantly when I was victimized. I was *that victim,* the one you dread ever entering your life or anyone else's, especially a child that can never understand adult situations. So along with accomplishment came confusion and unanswered questions for me. The ping-pong, puck-in-the-goal, back and forth was traumatizing. Higher highs and lower lows.

I don't want to cause any harm to my molester—no recognition for whom and what was done; no payback; no life's upheaval. It is strictly my intention to bring awareness to other childhood victims that have that lost, sick-feeling kid inside them and tell them that it can never be erased, but it can be *okay; it can get better; you can get past it.* No, it never goes away completely, the shadow of emotional turmoil will always be a part of you, but you can move on with your life. That's my biggest message to those who have suffered and lost their innocence way too soon.

As a result, I'm starting with this tough memory first. A relative touched me and had me touch them where a kid should not, where a kid just could never even begin to understand. I really didn't think to say anything about it because I didn't know how. *Why was I so afraid?* Because it was family, and my family, my parents and everybody else, were the best people a kid could have on his side. *How do you oust someone that is family?*

I never really found any answers to my questions, but at the time I knew it was something grownups did. Yet, I wish I'd had the courage to stand up and yell, scream, tell someone, but I didn't. I internalized it, as most children end up doing, therefore, blaming themselves. I should have said something. I was going to a religious school; I was an acolyte and an altar boy at mass. I knew as much right from wrong as any kid my age could. And, I knew it was wrong. I thought I was being brave for not saying anything, but I was really just too scared.

This type of trauma stays in your head at all times, even though I convinced myself that hockey put it in a place far away. I was able to keep it out of my thought processes for long periods, but it always returned; so, in actuality, it never really went anywhere. Consequently, with the first taste of success by achieving the initial stage of my dream, my brain gave me the intense desire to be the best-of-the-best at hockey, and I made the most concentrated effort possible at making my dream come true for the long haul, but little did I know I would need much stronger coping skills in the years ahead.

▪▪

I leave you with this last observation. It's freeing and comforting to know that you're not alone. I'm not happy other people have had to do through this, but I'm happy that I'm not some kind of weirdo and the only one who didn't say anything, didn't do anything, didn't tell. I may be a coward, but I've had to accept that it was the only choice I was comfortable with at that young, tender age.

Chapter Ten: Memories, *"What matters most and what defines us?"*

I want to mention here the testimonial/review by my friend Keith Zuccarelli that is at the beginning of this book. In your hurry to get to the meat of the story, you may have skipped his kind and inspiring letter. Keith was one of my best memories from High School. Be sure to read his words; they brought tears to my eyes.

I have so many memories of the Holy Name of Jesus School in New Rochelle. I remember silly and seemingly inconsequential things but looking back, everything had meaning and made me into the husband, father, and adult that I have become. It may have taken me a while to get to this place in my life with all I had to wade through, but I did reach this comfortable nostalgia in spite of myself!

I have to chuckle a little as I remember the teachers. Mr. D would grab a certain sensitive part of your elbow when you misbehaved, but instead of going to the principal and getting your parents involved with detention or being expelled, you had a really sore elbow for a short time and learned your lesson. You didn't want to get caught by Mr. D again.

Ms. Courtney had a real thing against wearing hats in the classroom. She displayed the confiscated hats as wall art. I lost some of my favorites caps by talking in the hallways of our hollowed building.

Sister Barbara was an enigma to me. Everyone was afraid of her. Maybe she just liked me, so I didn't see what she did or said to others. When it came down to it, she was just a nice old lady. I was glad to have her for my teacher.

Mr. Burwell was another odd teacher, but "odd" in a good sense. He was the Math teacher and would sing to us to help us learn our Math problems. Even today if I'm thinking of a silly rhyme or reading verse to my kids, I start singing and fondly remember my eighth-grade Math classroom.

Mrs. Spillet had so much patience with us unruly kids. I don't know how she did it, but she always had a smile for me every single day.

There are a few of these teachers and classmates as well that I "speak" with on social media. It has helped me deal with all my health and personal issues. They have given me invaluable insight into how I was as a student, an innocent time before everything started falling apart in my life.

One of my most favorite songs in the world is "Oh Holy Night" partly because it has such an endearing memory. Mr. Burwell would sing this song every year during the holidays. And did he *SING IT!* I would stop whatever I was doing

The thoughts in my head would disappear as if my magic, and my whole being would be immersed in the song and his voice. He could belt out that song like no one I've ever heard before or since! To this day, "Oh Holy Night" brings me peace and comfort. No matter where I hear it or who's singing it; it's always Mr. Burwell's voice that I hear in my mind, my heart, and my soul. I didn't realize the great significance it held for me until later in life. This realization became an important part of me being able to understand who I am and what soothes me when things seem to be too much to bear.

I really enjoyed being an acolyte in church. It was fun for me! Often, I had to serve mass early in the morning before school started. It was part of the culture of the times and the Catholic Church. Father Aufieri and Father Biglan were the two main Priests in our congregation. They were always available to answer questions from us kids in a way that we could understand—on our level, so to speak. They were masters at explaining and instilling wisdom in stubborn, hard-headed kids like me.

I know there are some bad feelings about the church in today's culture, but all of my memories are happy and positive. These childhood memories have been a quiet balm within me to survive all the turmoil I have had to endure. Maybe that was why I was able to escape from the dark secret inside me for weeks and months at a time. That and hockey!

These are the memories *"...that mattered most and defined me..."* as the man I am today.

Chapter Eleven: Hockey, *"Hockey was and still is my first true love!"*

The first year of making the hockey team was really a trial year, and it's the way in any sport or serious pursuit in which kids gets involved. Childhood is a time of learning skills and likes/dislikes that will follow us throughout our entire lives. We change and evolve and augment our desires as we mature, but the basic foundation is set into place by your family, your achievements, and unfortunately also your defeats.

I don't think anything ever hurts as much as the times you're denied something when you're young. By the same token, your successes are felt just as deeply. The excitement is the thing dreams are made of, and this was my dream! These are the things that we never forget. *"This is what we're really made of, and the team taught me much about life and people."*

Of course, if you don't *make the cut, go the distance, hang in there for the long haul with sports,* as with all extracurricular activities, there's a monetary investment from your parents. They had three kids to provide for, with only my dad working. Yeah, it was tough for him, but my folks never wanted to tell us we couldn't do something because of finances, but we knew *"money didn't grow on trees".*

When I was outside, my mode of transportation was roller blades, and I always had a hockey stick and gloves, just in case. Everything I did revolved around hockey, and my mom had to pry me off the streets every evening to get me in the house. But, of course, in the house I just ended up in the basement continuing to practice.

With me, there was never any question that I would ask Mom and Dad to *cut their losses* with hockey equipment and invest in something else, so I could try another sport. Gosh, it had been hard enough for me to make it this far *"Hockey was the only thing I wanted in my life!"*

The next year and each successive year, the doctors would continue to let me play as long as my medical tests came back perfectly healthy. Yeah, the heart murmur had to be monitored, but it wasn't stopping me from playing anymore.

***

When I was eleven years old—I know my parents had to scrimp and save for it—I started attending hockey camps every summer. It was just common sense, I guess, that if I was going to make this my life and play for the coveted New York Rangers, I needed to get better at hockey. Slamming into the boards to stop my forward motion was not the best way to improve my skating and playing skills.

With some specialized training provided at my first-ever hockey camp, I learned how to stop on a dime.

Going to hockey camps really gave me a new perspective on what I needed to correct and improve if I was going to make my dream a reality. And at this point it seemed that nothing could ever stop me.

This became the very air that I breathed, and I embraced it with an enthusiasm that I became known for at school and in my neighborhood. When anyone asked me what I wanted to do when I grew up, the answer was always the same ... *"Play professional hockey for the Rangers!"*

Each year after hockey camp, I came back with new ideas, new strategies, and complicated diagrams and breakdowns of how plays are set up, how passes are planned, and especially how goals are made. It's all geometric lines and players being at the right place at the right time, keeping in mind every second how fickle the ice can be with puck slides and hops and rough ice slowing the puck to a crawl or slick ice sending it soaring when you least expect it. The best rule-of-thumb is don't expect anything 'cause you never know for sure. I think that's the overall excitement of the game; that and the rapid action that only ice can deliver to both players and fans.

***

I approached my second season with much anticipation and fear. I knew the reason that I made the roster the year before was because I showed such love for the game—"heart" as my coaches called it—and I just wouldn't give up! I was terrified that this just wouldn't be enough to carry me through the rugged competition of making the cut again.

I had to prove myself to the coaches and exhibit a much stronger playing ability than I had the year before. I had to show them I knew the game and had what it took to make a difference for the whole team; there was just no other option for me. Teamwork and working together is paramount in hockey. There is no such thing as a one-man show in this sport!

I didn't sleep much for weeks before the tryouts. My nerves were so intense I was practically sick, but I knew I had to rest so I could be in tip-top performance. Every night I analyzed plays and passes and shots in my head, always making the impossible goals. I had to admit to myself that I was scoring more than last year, skating better, and I had become involved in more groups and practices and games. So, with each night that passed, I grew more confident, more convinced that I could do this, and the coaches would notice me as a solid, versatile player.

I also was hearing comments from not just family members, but other kids and grownups in my hometown. Everyone wanted me on their team! I certainly wasn't the biggest kid or oldest kid who played. In fact, I was small for my age, but

I was making an impression that remains with my former classmates and their families to this day.

I made the cut that second season, and it was one of my most favorite years playing hockey. I was living the dream and had found my true love. There were a lot of kids from my class and my neighborhood on the team, and we developed a close camaraderie that has stood the test of time. For many seasons to come, we would be united in the joy and passion of hockey; many of us remaining friends to this day.

By staying in touch with my hockey buddies, I've recently learned something else about myself that was so important in writing this book: *"I was always remembered as the kid who played his heart out on the hockey team and followed the New York Rangers as if they were my guiding light, which they were... That's how dreams are manifested. You have to believe in yourself, and I did ... to the point that it was never forgotten!"*

Testimonial by Kelly A. Hepburn

To know Anthony, is to truly love and be inspired by him. I was only seven years old when I realized I had a lifelong friend and confidant. His infectious, wide-eyed optimism beamed from him even as a boy. It was obvious even at a very young age that if Anthony set his sights on a goal, it was absolute that it would be achieved. Even during adolescence, Anthony was a known hockey success in and around our city and county. With that, he continued to persevere with xcellent grades, diligence, and dedication to land himself in a renowned reparatory school and achieve more greatness on an academic and sporting vel.

During the years we were separated, due to living on opposite sides of town and attending different schools, seeing him for the first time in a while felt like I had just seen him yesterday. Greeting him with an ear-to ear grin and a huge hug, it was like no time had passed at all. Back then, we didn't have the convenience of social media and networking. We had pagers, quarters, and a nearby payphone. The love and happiness that emanated from him was genuine and sincere. Anthony was truly happy to see his friends and the people he deeply cared about.

Since birth, Anthony struggled with some health conditions that nobody would ever know about, considering how steadfast he lived life. Grabbing any and every opportunity to be his best self, nothing in the world could stop him from achieving greatness.

Anthony has a tremendous love for his family and friends, a loyalty almost to a fault. I believe it was his way of giving back what his family had provided for him during the times he struggled in life. You could literally feel it from one hug from him. An embrace from Anthony was enough to make anyone who loved him or was loved by him forget about what was going on in their own lives. cherishing the life we do have. To see his bright eyes and passion considering the obstacles he overcame was inspiring to everyone, and still is to this day.

A lot of times with Anthony, it was like he was so concerned with making everyone around him feel loved that he forgot to love and care about himself. Empathetic and passionate towards the people he loved, he was blessed to receive that same love from his family. They were truly the lifeline for him that he had been for so many others. His mom and sisters, especially, showed tough love when needed, and appreciation and pride when deserved.

I personally watched Anthony flourish into the incredible man he is today, a man that lets nothing stand in his way of achieving his dreams. Over the years he immersed himself into several different lifestyles and adapted with ease. He just strides along rolling with the punches and growing with them. It is with great pride and honor that I can watch my friend achieve yet another goal with Fuzzy Logic. Watching Anthony balance family life and his passions is truly beautiful and inspiring.

If there is anything I have learned from my friend, it is to love with your whole heart; accept the world as it may be; and to never let anything stand in the way of your goals and dreams. He taught me that the power of changes lays within you, and only you. All you have to do is be bold enough to dig in and grab the will.

I'm so proud of you my dear friend, and I will continue to support you as you have always supported me. In my bright and dark days, you've never turned your back and I believe with my whole heart you never will. Don't ever stop being you and keep gifting the world by shining your light on all of us.

Anthony, I love and admire you always.

Your dear friend, Kelly A Hepburn

Chapter Twelve: Living the Dream, *"My life was perfect, wasn't it?"*

The summer was rapidly approaching after my 3rd season of playing hockey and the end of my 8th grade year. Beginning high school next year at a new school and playing hockey at a higher level consumed me. Everything was going wonderfully. I was an integral and, in some cases, idolized member of the New Rochelle Lightning Hockey Team, proving that I could move as fast as lightning and score! Every year my blood tests and physical exams had been passed with flying colors. Nothing could stop me now; I was *"living my dream."*

My parents asked me if I wanted to go to a 6-week summer hockey camp. To me, it sounded like heaven. My parents were stretched for money with a growing family and limited income, so this wasn't a way to get rid of me for the summer as the only rowdy boy in the family. You hear about that kind of *"babysitter"* in our modern society where both parents work or socialize on a large scale. Looking back, though, I'm sure my mom could definitely use the rest, not having to worry about me bashing my head and face on the blacktop road in front of our house while on roller blades and fighting over a puck.

Surprisingly, my parents didn't actually know much about hockey. They asked me more questions about the sport than I ever asked them. I can only give you *"a wink and a chuckle"* with this acknowledgement. They were just too busy to learn about it and take it as seriously as I did. And, they trusted me.

I had never been away from home and my family this long before, so it did cause me some anxious moments. I was also concerned about, *"What if the other kids don't like me?"* It wasn't like being on the team with all my friends and buddies. My parents could come visit me on the weekends, which they did every weekend because on the second week I broke down and cried because I was one of the smallest and youngest boys at the camp, but mainly I was just plain homesick.

Somewhere in the midst of all this, however, things started to change. It didn't happen in a single, earth-shattering moment but snuck up on me without any conscious realization on my part or anyone else's, for that matter. Not even my parents were aware that something was brewing inside me that would disrupt my perfect world, my dream. This was a subtle, devastating new obstacle for me that we would face as a family and overcome, like all the rest. *"Was this one more story to tell on my way to become the best hockey player to ever lace up a pair of ice skates or was it another nightmare that I would have to be pulled out of because couldn't save myself?*

I'm going to back up a little bit to give you the full story that leads up to this crisis.

***

It was the last school trip of the year, and my class was going on a trip to Playland, also known as Rye Playland. This "old in amusement but young in enthusiasm" American Premier Playground dates back to 1928 in Westchester County. It features Art Deco buildings, the beach, a fishing pier, and "ice!" on Long Island Sound. Many of the rides and attractions are originals or reproductions from the very first 1928 masterpieces. The Dragon Coaster is known worldwide as a wooden roller coaster in a time when all others have met their demise. They had just added the Log Flume ride before our school trip to accommodate more modern technology for the hot, humid summers. To me, however, I was psyched up because it was famous for being the New York Rangers practice facility.

There is one memory that sticks in my mind even today. Antonia Rossi and I were getting ready to try the new Log Flume ride. Antonia was one of my best friends. I was able to confide almost anything to her, and I trusted her opinions, listening to what she had to say at a time when I didn't really listen to anybody. We got on the ride, buckled ourselves in, and about 30 seconds later she turned to me and said I looked pale. *"Do you feel alright, Anthony?"*

I didn't really think anything of it. I wasn't feeling my normal 100% ball of energy and jokester sarcasm, but it was odd for someone to tell me I was pale. I mean, everyone knew that tanning wasn't my strong point, nor could I ever maintain a tan all summer like a lot of my friends. Yet, there was truth behind this comment of Antonia's; after all she knew me very well. I wasn't myself, but there were really no visible signs that anything was wrong. So, this comment had no real meaning for me until … well, until I had to try and piece together what was happening to me.

The whole class enjoyed our day at the park, and when the day was done, we returned home in high spirits, but my demeanor was a little sluggish. On the weekends, we had roller hockey tournaments at Stephenson Park in New Rochelle. I would always be there, of course, but on this particular weekend, I didn't have the same energy in the game that I usually had. Again, I thought nothing of it. I drank more water, so I could keep on playing. Nothing was going to stop me!

These weekend tournaments were done in playoff format. After two losses a team would be eliminated. This was more to claim bragging rights than anything else … *you had to be the last team standing!* My best friend *"Spanky"* was on the team I was playing against. If anyone knew what I was made of as a hockey player, it was Spanky. All I remember about that day is that I lined up a slapshot and it was beautiful. I placed it right under the top crossbar. I remember hearing the smack of the plastic and knew it went in—*GOAL!*—but things were looking a little fuzzy.

Suddenly, my legs felt heavy and weak, my eyesight was blurry, and I totally collapsed immediately after taking the shot. I do remember seeing the look on Spanky's face, and it was enough for me to know that something was really wrong. I had to be helped off the pavement, still in my roller blades, to sit beside my mom who as always was a spectator cheering me on. I weakly said to my mother, *"I just don't feel right."*

We stayed until the game was over—I insisted—but mom was on the phone with the doctors immediately after we got home. I tried to listen to the conversation but I just stayed on the couch. I didn't have the energy to move closer to the phone to hear what was being said. There was a lot going on in our family at this time. My niece had just been born, and my mom was working during the day. Michelle, my oldest sister, offered to take me to the doctor to get my blood checked and see if this was related to the heart murmur. No biggie; this was all routine for me.

It did seem a little odd to me that I felt lightheaded after the nurse drew blood. That had never happened before. She got me some orange juice. This blood test would change my future forever. We had just left the doctor's office to go home and await the verdict of the blood chemistry—me, Michelle, and baby Elizabeth who my sister was holding. I didn't remember how I felt right after the blood was drawn, and that was odd too. We were in the elevator when everything went black. I don't remember anything after that. I guess from what bystanders witnessed, I exited the elevator under my own power. I just remember coming to in the hallway with a bunch of people around me. *"How had I gotten here?"*

When I headed down the hall to exit the building, I collapsed again face-first into the double doors, but I really don't remember that either. Michelle, on the other hand, has this image burnt in her brain; she's never forgotten it. She told me my face hit the glass, slid down the slick translucent surface, and the door to the outside opened from my deadweight impact. Since Michelle was holding Elizabeth, she couldn't do anything for me. She started screaming for help, but I didn't hear a thing. The next thing I remember is a lady, a nurse I guess, holding my chin over a white bucket that I was throwing up into while she rubbed my head. She kept telling me I was going to be okay. I'd been moved out of the doorway and into the hall. I do remember my eyes just wouldn't focus. I was confused, and a new feeling was surfacing. One I had never felt before. *I was scared for the first time in my life!*

After we got home, my mom was there, and I could see the worry on her face as she talked to the doctor on the phone. I'd never heard Mom sound like that before. The problem causing all her concern was me—I was totally helpless—I just kept going over this again and again in my head. Afterwards, Mom came over to me on the couch and said, *"We will figure this out."* She was so caring and loving, I wanted to cry, but I was still confused. *Figure what out? This was just another obstacle in my path, right? I'd get through this like I'd gotten through everything else.* But my mom's facial expression said something different.

Initially, they thought it was cancer, but they couldn't be sure. The blood tests weren't giving any definitive answers, but the symptoms were full of doom and gloom. I kept thinking that my really important 6-week hockey camp was just a few weeks away. I had to get better! I didn't have time to be a *"victim"*. I'd never been a victim! This was unfair and just not an option for me. *"I HAD TO FULFILL MY DREAM! I HAD TO PLAY HOCKEY!"*

Even at this young age, I focused only on healing and continuing my life, my dream, of playing hockey. This is how I had faced everything since I was only eight years old. It was the same discipline and dedication that I mentally prepared myself for to make the team and play hockey, pursuing my dream. *"Everything was supposed to be perfect, wasn't it? What happened and when did it happen and why?"*

I was finally diagnosed with severe iron deficiency anemia. The next few weeks were hell and involved many trips to the doctor to get booster shots in my thighs. To paint the picture, it was like someone igniting a cigarette lighter, heating it up, and sticking it directly into my thigh muscles. The only difference was there weren't any scars to leave a telltale trace. It took about three weeks for my body to heal, but there was never an explanation as to why it had happened. I was cleared to attend hockey camp and that's all that mattered to me. I had always healed quickly, so that had to be the answer. I said my prayers and thanked the Lord that I was okay … again.

It seemed at the time that I just took everything in stride, calmly and optimistically, but thinking about it now as an adult, it was the same coping mechanism I used to deal with being molested. I hid behind my mask what I was really feeling and ignored the bigger picture. *Again, why didn't I ask more questions? Why didn't I take it more seriously? I just wanted to forget about it, like I did the molestation that I had never, ever shared with anyone.*

Hockey was my getaway and my salvation, but it was also my scapegoat; the one that hid the true answers not just from my family and my friends, but from myself,

This hockey camp turned out to be one of the best I ever attended, but it didn't give me any downtime to rest and recuperate from the full season of hockey that had just ended, followed by a blood disease that was never quite understood and then rigorous hockey every day for a month-and-a-half. And what was I coming back to? Fall and hockey tryouts again, but this time in high school where the competition would be stiffer.

The final Friday before the last game of hockey camp, another incident occurred. I can *kind of recall* the impact as I blacked out and hit the boards. Th coaches told me what happened afterwards because again, I didn't quite remember it all. It was like I was experiencing an entirely different reality that no one could see or believe but me. For a split second, I saw my niece's face as a reflection from the doctor's appointment where my weak, thin blood had been drawn, but it was the coach's face above me. He checked me over as they do: *"Can you feel your arms, your legs? Does anything hurt?"* No, I told them, and I asked for someone to help me up. I was able to skate off the ice under my own power, but I was really groggy on the bench.

The next day I wanted to play, but there was a huge bruise on the right side of my neck. It was Friday, so my parents would be there on Saturday like every other weekend. This was going to take a lot of explaining to justify to my mom and dad. It looked like someone had hit me with a baseball bat. I decided *not* to call my parents on Friday night. Time enough to face them when they came to watch my last game and then take me home after the camp ended. I knew this wasn't going to be easy. When they arrived the next day, they were immediately requested to go to the main office before they had even seen me.

When my parents joined me, Dad seemed unphased, but Mom said, *"What he hell did you do?"* The coaches had reiterated the story of what happened to hem; everyone was concerned. My mom and dad looked at me with weak smiles. got to give them credit for that, supporting me right, wrong, or indifferent. They sked me what I wanted to do, and I said, *"Play,"* of course. Yeah, I could have ›een hurt much worse, but who thinks of that when there's hockey to play? Certainly not me.

With that memorable last game at camp, my parents let me make my own lecision whether to play or not. They had always morally guided my decisions and ›ehavior, but when it came to hockey, they always asked me what it was I wanted to achieve. They provided me with every opportunity to grow and experience life on its own terms, in spite of my medical history, but they let *me call the shots*. There is only one way to really grow, and that is to learn from your own personal experiences. Through their faith in me, it allowed me to honestly understand the seriousness of the situation with the severe anemia condition still fresh in all of our minds.

I thank my parents for allowing me to make that choice even though they were extremely concerned when they arrived at the camp to be told I had almost blacked out yet again. A lot was happening that summer concerning me, my sisters who were now adults, and my parents. They had just become grandparents, and I was just getting ready to begin high school.

What they didn't know, however, was that I tucked another major life event in some secret, secluded spot of my subconscious. It was the way I handled everything by simply not acknowledging or accepting it. I didn't have time to worry about the *"small stuff"*. But now, 20 years later, as I'm revisiting these events,

DO remember thinking, *"I'm living the dream, and my life was perfect, wasn't it?*

I would pay dearly for these delusions when it all came crashing down. My parents

with letting me make the choice on that all important final game were believing in

me. I can never thank them enough for their faith in me, whether I deserved it or

not.

Chapter Thirteen: High School Hockey, *"Making my own decisions."*

Due to my success in hockey through middle school, my parents and I had been talking about a major decision for me the whole second half of my 8th grade year at Holy Name of Jesus School in New Rochelle. I could attend either Iona Preparatory School or New Rochelle High School. One memory from before the spring and the end of our hockey season that year had to do with the rink at Rye Playland. This rink is about half the size of the main arena and was used by smaller kids to practice so that public skating and practice for the older kids wouldn't have to alternate as much with so many rotating hockey teams needing time on the ice.

Mom took me to practice because Dad, of course, was working. It was before practice because the bigger kids were still on the ice for their assigned practice time. I was scared to play against older kids, but when embroiled in the depths of competition and the excitement of the game my fear actually fueled me onto greatness. I was making a name for myself to the point that I'd started to believe myself invincible, but I still had my doubts when it came to the unpredictability of the ice. I thought my reputation came from the roller hockey tournaments.

You can tell this all happened before the anemia that stopped me in my tracks, months later in the early part of the summer. This memory is so clear in my adult mind. I saw a coach there at the Rye Playland smaller rink for whom I had great admiration. He came up to my mom and me and asked to speak with us. He'd evidently been watching my growth as a hockey player this whole 3rd season that I played for the New Rochelle Lightning Hockey Team. At the time I didn't realize that I had been making a name for myself not just in roller hockey, but ice hockey as well.

The coach approached us with a big smile on his face and asked me, "Are you ready for Varsity Hockey?" For an 8th grader, this was like telling me I'd just won the lottery. It was an extreme honor and you had to have really excellent ability to play Varsity Hockey as a freshman. I wasn't even a freshman yet! I knew this wasn't offered to very many hockey players from any team, and the New Rochelle Lightning wasn't that big of a team. *"He'd been following my progression as an ice hockey player? Wow! This is how my dream always came to fruition in my imagination, but this was really happening! I repeat, WOW!"*

I also knew that being a freshman on the Varsity team could cause some friction with existing players who had to fight to retain their positions. But in spite of the heady feeling of accomplishment that was reeling through my mind, I floored the coach and probably my mom too when I said, "Sorry, Coach, I'm going to Iona."

I'd been really thinking about this and talking to my parents. Until I said that, though, I hadn't realized I'd made a definite decision. My parents had agreed that it was my choice to make because I needed to base it on what I wanted to see happen on my path to the New York Rangers. They believed in me!

The coach glared at my mom with a confused look and then back at me as if I'd just stabbed him in the heart. I have no idea why I made that choice in that split second, but it just seemed right. I didn't know what the future held for me. I had my dream, and it hadn't changed. I was convinced I was going to play professional hockey for the New York Rangers. I was going to be one of the greats.

It really didn't matter which high school I attended. I was going to get there just the same. This coach who believed I was ready for Varsity Hockey at New Rochelle High School only halfway through my 8th grade year, made me believe for the first time that I really was going to be an ice hockey professional.

Looking back, I don't know, nor will I ever know, if I was making a sacrifice for a better education or simply *"making my own decision"*. I'm not really sure why I even said that, but I'd always liked doing the unexpected and unpredictable Maybe in nutshell, that was why that *"decision"* surfaced when it did. Who knows

The rest is history, as the cliché goes. And it really didn't make a difference in the grand scheme of things nor was it the missing piece of the puzzle that was my life.

***

After the fact and again since I've been an adult, I went over the reasons I made the split-second decision I'd made about high school and my dreams for the future. All of these factors were discussed at length in my household, but it needs to be shared here with the events that have made me the man I am today.

New Rochelle, of course, was a public high school where the majority of my friends and classmates, including the guys on the hockey team, would be attending. Iona Preparatory was different—a private, all-boys school that could provide a better education and more recognition for my dream of becoming a professional, well-balanced New York Rangers hockey player. It's no secret that my parents wanted me to focus on hockey. Perhaps, they figured if I went to high school with all of my friends, I might stray from the intended path that *everyone* expected me to follow. But they never said anything; they let me make my own decision.

I didn't know how my folks felt about my choice. They let me be me. I mean, how much control do we really have over our own destiny, our own journey? What is set in stone, left to chance, pre-arranged, manipulated by others, or altered right in the middle of what we perceive at the time is a positive change or a negative epercussion? I know these types of questions have no answers, and we really don't

now the full scope of our actions sometimes until time plays out the full scenario.

Of course, we never know when one begins or ends or even is postponed for further

levelopment.

Chapter Fourteen: Journey, *"If we saw the path, would it matter?"*

Just like previous events in my life, I never backtracked or second-guessed my decision once it was made. It was set in stone as far as I was concerned. There was no future in re-evaluating the path or the encounters that had led me to what had chosen. It was all part of the magic too of living the dream. My future was laid out before me, and I was going to play hockey.

The next chapter was beginning, and it was high school and, of course, hockey! I would play high school hockey throughout my 17th year of age—through my senior year.

It doesn't seem that long ago, but the world and communication changes so fast now. It makes your head spin whether you're prepared for it or not. I'm not that old, but not that young, I guess, but social media didn't have the hold on us kids back then like it does today. Internet was a slow-moving, dial-up system. There were no Smart Phones yet. The coolest thing there was ... was a "Pager". Lol Some people may ask what a Pager is? ... Wow, times have changed!

Some people may wonder how they ever truly lived without the technology of today, which will be updated even by tomorrow. Gosh, it will be brand new 60 seconds from now! You always hear on the path of life the only constant is change.

And everything changes around us whether we like it or not. From the 90s on, we've ALL been growing up in the boom of technology. Regardless of your age, job, skill set, avocation or vocation. It's just the way it is, and we have to live with it. But that's okay! If you don't like today, tomorrow will be totally different.

I'm not going to bore you with silly high school stories. We can hear them on any street corner, in the subway, online, and especially from our parents. Yeah, I'll share a couple of things that are real standouts, but none of the transitions and changes that made up my high school hockey years deflated my dream or changed my mind. I was solid! Really, ask my family? I was going to be the best hockey player who ever lived!

***

At this point in my growth, this is how I felt. No bones about it. Everything I did revolved around hockey, and I just hid all the stuff that came before and after. It wasn't a concern. It wasn't important … not my health, not the molestation, not which school I went to or who my friends were … *nada, nothing, incognito… hockey player in training.* That was the path and it wouldn't matter if it changed, I'd still get there.

I know now that I was fortunate to attend an excellent place like Iona and that my parents could afford to send me to that caliber of private, intimate, educational instruction. It was dreamlike too in a magical sort of way.

Okay, I'll admit I was insecure about going to a new school where I really didn't know anybody. But I was lucky! In the first few days at Iona Prep, I found my best friend, Keith Zuccarelli, who would be my best friend through high school and beyond, up to and including today. We had Homeroom together and most of our classes. It was destined, just like my dream.

We have all kinds of funny stories, but he also brought me into a second family. And he's living his dream now too. A radio show! We both liked the "shock Jock" variety of broadcasting in high school. The laughs never stopped for us. He went through a bad time after his father died, and we really don't speak of this today, too hard for him, but he sent me a beautiful message on how much our friendship helped him through that incomprehensible ordeal. This is sort of funny because I never remember telling him how much the friendship meant to me. He just knew!

I played freshman hockey, but it was my sophomore year that sparked the realization that my dream was very much alive and still on-track. I was still attending hockey camps every summer, thanks to my parents and their belief in my destiny, and I was growing not so much physically, but mentally. I think everyone goes through this transition in high school, but mine was extra important. It had nothing to do with my health, the heart murmur, the anemia, or my carefully guarded secrets. I had a lot more to juggle, but it was giving me new-found confidence and increasing my success on the ice. Popularity came with it. That was an amazing perk!

This is about the time I met Brother Gaffney, who would play a critical role for me during my entire education at Iona Prep. At first, I didn't even understand the effect he would have on my life. *"So why should the path matter on the journey? Well, believe me, it just does..."*

I don't even know who noticed it first, him or me, and the day or moment it happened is of no consequence. A special bond was forged between us when I saw him standing at the end of the bench cheering me on with the hockey team. Wow! He was incredible! He wasn't screaming at me like most of the other kids' parents, and he almost always had something positive to say to me. The criticisms and yelling were left to the coaches. That's what they're for, after all, but Brother Gaffney brought a calming influence when I really needed it. There was always so much noise, pushing and shoving, and just doing *boy-things.*

Looking back, it's like it's in slow motion when a connection occurs. People find their mental balance in the oddest ways—through an animal, a pet; at a place real or imaginary; by meditating to the sounds of the ocean; or something a predictable in my childhood/teen years as going to confession regularly. I didn't have a situation or problem that the sound of Brother Gaffney's voice couldn't help me resolve mentally: Comfort, love, affinity and dedication for my wellbeing and my mind. It was all part of the dream.

At a particular opportune time, which only Brother Gaffney could discern, he would request for me to give him a *"word"*. He would seek me out for this. And the words were always a positive reinforcement. Don't know how it happened or where it came from, but he became my good luck charm when he bestowed on me his nickname. One word, one interjection, by Brother Gaffney at the end of my sophomore year in which we had an outstanding team, and we fell just shy of winning the Catholic High School Championship.

He had pulled me aside, looked directly in my eyes and said, "I believe in you, Glyder." I looked at him kind of funny, I'm sure, when I asked, "Who's *Glyder*?" He looked deep into my eyes again, so I knew he wasn't kidding, and was serious when he said, "Why you are, now *lead your team...* " Talk about the stuff that dreams are made of!

For the rest of my time at Iona, on or off the ice, Brother Gaffney was always the same man ... kind, loving, faithful, and inspiring. I would always have someone to confide in throughout high school, and I always knew there was someone who believed in me, even when there were times when it seemed like no one else would.

This is the story I want to leave you with that shows beyond a shadow of a doubt that *"It **DOES** matter where you are on the path, regardless of what the journey holds for you down the road."*

SECTION IV

Transitions of Upheaval

"I knew everything wouldn't be easy, but gimme' a

break!"

Chapter Fifteen: From High School, *"Was this the hardest? Yeah…"*

"I would tell anyone who wants to follow their dreams that you need to get comfortable with being uncomfortable."

—Anthony J. Williams, III, author "On Borrowed Time, The Reinvention of a Lost Soul"

Things are really different today. Social media has really *upped the exposure* for everyone, even everyday people, not just *"major sports stars"*. Not so, when I was in high school. To get noticed you had to be in the newspapers, on the local news, but also there was this little window of opportunity, which was the short time in which the game was played, as opposed to all the prep work. This was when the majority of recruiters, scouts, and journalists were there watching … *me!*

Since my reason for telling my story is to help others, I want to make two points upfront. It isn't the physical attributes that warranted more work, it was the mental that needed strengthening. I have just realized this in retrospect. And, back then, it depended which school you attended since there was only word-of-mouth and news stories, not Social Media platforms. I hope these two points, which I never considered at the time, will address the issues people have with well … **ALL** the concerns I talk about in this book.

***

Leading up to my junior year of high school, I was approached by one of my coaches who wanted me to attend a private school in Rhode Island. It seemed counterproductive to me at the time because I was already attending Iona, the premiere Catholic High School in my area of New York. Afterall, I wanted to play for the New York Rangers, right?

The anemia hadn't resurfaced; the heart murmur was a non-issue but being watched; and my junior and senior years of high school were my best years for making the TV news, the newspaper, and being scouted by recruiters. In my mind, *"It was a cinch!"*

The first time I had to re-evaluate my future—actually there were two instances—was when I suffered injuries during the game. One of them though, in particular, made me question my dream on a conscious level. I didn't talk about it. The same pattern of hiding deep concerns from myself kicked in with ferocious fervor. *Denial, bigtime!*

Playing in a game for the Junior B Ramapo Rangers, I went to get the puck from a defensive corner, and it hopped over my stick, so I turned toward the boards exposing my back. I thought I had enough time before the other team would press with a fore-check attack. Misjudgment is an understatement; the attack was already in-play, and I was blind to it. The lights went out!

There was a little peace as I lay on the ice blacked out, and then confusion when I regained consciousness and say my parents' faces. Dad walked me to the locker room to change and carry my hockey bag to the car. They kept me awake, asked me questions, did all the right things. This one was minor one, however. Every athlete faces injury and friction along the way. You become a star by overcoming obstacles, temptations, addiction.

My BIG obstacle came in a close game. *I got the puck on a fore-check and go to the back of the net till help, my guys, can arrive, but two opponents jump me. I slip between them, so I don't get hit on both sides. Only there's no room left behind the net. I collide into the net. My hip pad slips to the side, and my hip hits flush with the metal post. My leg goes numb. I try to get up. Nothing... But somehow, I struggle to the bench. I have to push through. My teammates open the bench door as I hobble over. In the locker room, Dad helps me get undressed, then dressed in street clothes carries my bag to the car. Now, it's like I'm living it all again, as I have in my mind so many times. No pain that night; just afterwards.*

A severely bruised hip flexor, but I was only out for three weeks before started practicing again. This was a test for me to reach out and feel the touch o my emotions when I was not playing hockey. That was my last obstacle in high school besides fights over ex-girlfriends.

Chapter Sixteen: To College, *"What was I supposed to do? I was lost!"*

I can't really tell you when it all started to fall apart. There were so many factors involved, and I don't think I was even cognizant of them or how long I'd been hiding these little jabs from myself. This Super Hero was the master of deception. Let's just say, they were adding up and crushing the life out of me.

Yet, on a conscious level, there just wasn't any room in my mind for worrying about kid-stuff. All I concentrated on was playing hockey, so I could play more hockey!

Girlfriends came and went in my life, blurring together, and friends did the same. I just wasn't paying attention. Now, as an adult, I am deeply saddened for all the people I took for granted. It definitely was a huge mistake for me to forget all my relationships and friendships. *Yeah, you read that right—"all of them!" I was going to be a hockey star, so I pushed my supporters right into the gutter.* **I was selfish.**

I mean, to be fair to myself, most high school friendships and especially "puppy love" relationships run the normal course—*there's that undefinable word again, "normal". Who's normal? Certainly **not** my normal.*

The bonds of school just naturally wither in the majority of people's lives with no hard feelings because life moves on. Everyone is heading for this college or that college, and that job or this vocation *rules* with pie-in-the-sky ambition. When you're a teen/young adult, you accept college as the most crucial period of your life—*I mean, that's what everybody tells ya'*—and decisions made at this time reach far into your future, affecting absolutely everything. And I don't disagree with that. Yet, in hindsight, it's *not* your entire life. It's really just a blip on the overall map of things. You have a chance, at a later date, to use those "do-overs, respawns, health packs, hints, guidance," literally or figuratively, that I mentioned in the Introduction, which are all part of the game. *You aren't stuck, and nothing is set in stone; no matter how much your parents and society want you to believe it is.*

That's where I disconnected. I *perceived* myself as stuck, whether I was or not. My options, in my mind, had all been taken from me, and it had nothing to do with choices. *That's when I lost my way.*

***

Don't get me wrong, I had some pretty good stuff going for me as well. I was the first ever in my family to graduate from a highly rated prep school like Iona. It was a big deal in my family, and I was proud. This was probably the first time I ever remember feeling pride for something besides hockey. *But would it also be my last?* Sometimes I feel that way… even today.

Yeah, I had everything figured out, just like every other sports jock says he does. I was meeting with scouts, recruiters, visiting colleges, and going through the motions that would take me onto the next leg of my dream. I was ready to take on anything and everything that came my way. *Look out world, here I come!*

These feelings of commitment and accomplishment, however, didn't last very long. I probably missed out on some real joyful experiences—the kind you feel where you're walking on air or floating in the clouds—because I didn't allow myself to engage these emotions. I always wanted more. Nothing was ever good enough. I moved like an addict from one heady feeling to another, never fully tasting the depth of my mood. ***I was shallow.***

When college didn't go as planned, I did what every other shallow person does. I gave up. I quit. I left after only one year. I wasn't disciplined enough to handle the stress of life *and* be a hockey professional at the same time. I lost my dream to my own low opinion of myself. The crowds weren't cheering anymore. So how could I drum up some excitement? There had to be a way—I was a star!

I wanted to have fun and laugh it up like the class clown I'd always been. I wanted to make others laugh and be the center of attention. Like a hockey player with an adoring audience! But without the proper support and guidance of my family as well as the newsworthy item that I had always been, I went totally *off the rails.*

The rude awakening was when I got into trouble and didn't know how to handle it. I decided to go home, regroup, and make a new plan with an easy walk-on program for hockey (The Rangers) or realize my dream by going undrafted. Either way, I knew I'd make it. I was destined for this; it's all there was in my mind; I was the *"Star"* Super Hero; my ego said, *"This is gonna happen because everything else has happened."* Good analysis? Hmm? *"Yeah, no…"*

Well, neither of these ideas worked out. It seemed like the deck was stacked against me. Doubt became all that was fused in my brain. Granted, I was still hiding things from myself, but the day-to-day was surfacing with way too much reality.

My parents had already decided that when I started college and their wild-child was settled, they were going to sell the house in New Rochelle and move to Dutchess County, New York. My sister Tara already lived up there, and Michelle and her husband Gabby weren't far behind them. They still traveled back and forth to New York for work, up until August of 2001. A month later, on September 11th, 2001, New York would become Ground-Zero for the terrorist attack on The Twin Towers that rocked everybody's world and has remained so until this day.

By the time I "bombed out" of college, the home I planned to go back to wasn't even there. I was a lost little boy with lots of problems; everything was falling apart all around me.

"So, tell me, what was I supposed to do?"

My dream died in the rubble and the dust.

Chapter Seventeen: After It All Fell Apart, *"My family, yours too…"*

We were all numb. How could we be anything else? We didn't know it was coming. We didn't know who was at fault, not at first. I think it was so unbelievable, those first few moments of denial—because we had nothing with which to compare this atrocity. We pulled together as a country, but we were struck dumb. We couldn't even talk.

I know I forgot about my personal issues … at first. I'm not even sure when reality started to surface … for anyone. It was devastation and destruction and lists of people for which everyone was looking. The trauma, the drama, the pain. No one knew what to do. My family didn't know what to do. *And neither did yours! I can bet my life on that one…*

Hockey, the Rangers. For once I didn't even think about that. I don't know what I thought about. Was I hiding things from myself again? Was everyone in America thinking it was just a bad dream, and we'd wake up and everything would be back the way it was supposed to be?

I'd just left college. It was supposed to be the beginning … not the end. So, what was coming next? Was there more to come? No one knew. We were all whirling in confusion, doubt, disbelief. For once, I was no exception.

I know; I know. I said I was selfish, and I am. So somewhere along the way, thought of me. Somewhere, sometime, somehow.

***

So where were you when the world fell apart? Everyone remembers exactly what they were doing and how they found out—what time it was; what day it was; what date it was; what they had for breakfast; who they called first; how hands slipped up to cover their mouths as they whispered, "Oh, my God!" ("OMG" was not yet popular…)

Okay, so everybody is watching, and then the brave people crashing into the helicopter pad of The Pentagon. Live, on TV, right in front of our eyes. *What did we all do?*

By now, those of you who are remembering where they were and what they were doing … well, I **am** the exception. *Aren't I always?* I really don't remember everything in vivid detail like everybody else. I don't know why. Shock? Selfish? Numbness? I call it "unexpressed emotion". I'd been living it for so long, it was second nature. Hide from what you can't face … *Boom! Done!*

I'm going to have to skip ahead a little bit. I had to go back and ask my family what they were doing; where they were; what they remembered. We had all just moved. I moved with them. *I mean, where else was I going to go?* As my saving grace, if I hadn't already have left college, I would have left at this juncture anyway. *Wouldn't you? Maybe not. Maybe you're made of sterner stuff...*

When it all falls apart, all that's left is family and love.

OMG, hasn't it taken me a long enough to realize this basic truth?

These are my transitions up to this point. And I'll get back to being that lost, selfish, frightened, abused child in an 18-year old's body. *Life goes on for some of us, except for all those who died.*

Chapter Eighteen: Trying Again, *"What's a backup plan and why?"*

I wasn't able to backup, retrieve the puck off the boards and fickle ice, and fire a goal so fast and perfect off the end of my stick that no goalie could ever begin to stop it. I didn't have a plan in place to transition my life, so warning bells and goal foghorns went unnoticed. There were no roaring crowds jumping to their feet and cheering. There were no agents, recruiters, scouts, or journalists.

At 18 years old, I was a *"has been"* who just hadn't been able to make it. I like to think there were extenuating circumstances, but that wasn't really the case, either. And it was all my own stupid, egotistical fault. A rude awakening, to say the least, once the smoke had cleared, and it was time to look ahead to figure out what came next. There was no contingency plan.

Literally everything in my mind had been centered around my dream of being a professional hockey player for the Rangers for so long, there wasn't anything else to fall back on or aspire to. A dream has to be nurtured, believed in, be all encompassing and time/energy-consuming. *But what if the dream falls apart too?*

When everything else fell apart, I lost all the familiar faces I was used to when my entire family moved to upstate New York. I wasn't at all financially stable, so the idea of living on my own was out of the question. Since I had concentrated *only on hockey,* I didn't have the skill-sets in place for any other areas of my life. I didn't think I needed anything else. *"Boy, was I ever wrong!"*

***

As I mentioned, there was no one to blame but myself. I didn't know what I else I could conquer, what else I could do, what else I could study. Iona had always made those decisions for me. So, my parents suggested I go to the local community college in upstate New York to see what would spark my interest in another field of endeavor. They were doing what parents are supposed to do, and the whole family was in on this together.

Had to be something else, right? I was a smart kid; I made things happen; I had never let my family down before, nor had they ever stopped believing in me. To them, this was just a little set-back. To me? It seemed like the end of the world.

I developed a rigid attitude—*a chip on my shoulder*—and didn't care about anything anymore, but I didn't need to tell my family that, *now did I?* I was hiding my feelings of inadequacy just like I'd always done before. *No big deal!* I was the good son, followed everyone's advice, and went through the motions of my family's suggestions.

They didn't need to know that my heart wasn't in it. They didn't need to know anything about what I was going through. I'd been quiet about the fact that I'd been molested for what … decades? So, the same song played over and over … more secrets, more omissions, more jokes that fell on deaf ears. *Was I really kidding anyone else? Was anyone even listening? Listening to what? I wasn't saying nothin'!*

***

I attended Duchess Community College for a few semesters, taking core classes with no brainstorms surfacing to point me towards a Major in another field of study. My parents and sisters, even my brothers-in-law, let me make my own decisions as the rest of the family had always allowed me to do. Besides, they had their own *stuff* they were dealing with, as was the rest of the country, the rest of world.

I've admitted a lot of internal dialogue here—some of which I hid even from myself—but I bet others have done this kind of thing too. *Why talk about things that have no future? Why even bother with a backup plan, when it just gets torn up, thrown out, and changed anyway? I mean, why; just tell me why?*

It's only in reflection that I can start to find a "why". I may not even have the answer yet, but I know somewhere along the road to destruction, there has to be a "why"; just as along the road to greatness, there has to be a "why" and a "how".

"That's the things that dreams are made of," I spit out in sarcasm at this transition. *"Check with me later to see if my opinion has changed."*

Before we embark on the next leg of this journey together, let's think about our families. The families who love us, and the families we love. How much we rely on each other. And I've got to tell you … ***MINE WAS THE ABSOLUTE BEST!***

I can see heads shaking up and down, *"Yes, yes, yes!"* all across this beautiful country of ours. All of our families are the best, even if it isn't perfect, even if it's downright ugly, even if we can't define it. There's always a moment in time when we have the very, very best to reach out for and capture. That's what makes us strong! That's what allows us to go on in the face of adversity.

Our country was at war. I was at war with myself. My family? … well, that's the next section.

SECTION V

A Step Back in Time...

"The best support group ever; did I appreciate it?

Nope!"

Chapter Nineteen: Godmother Aunt Sue, *"Tried to chang[e] my life."*

Testimonial by 'Aunt Sue': Well, it certainly is easy for me to write about my Godson. Being asked to be Anthony's Godmother was a gift I will always be so thankful for. Anthony has many great qualities, but by far the best thing about Anthony is his zest for life. He lit up a room when he walked into it. There was always  something special about him; I knew he was destined to do great things.

I once entered him in an American Boy Contest. The prize was som[e] scholarship money, and I thought that was great so off we went to the hotel for th[e] weekend. When we got there, I saw all the kids clearly had been professionall[y] coached, and I figured we were way out of their league.

Anthony was only 11 years old; the others were in that age range too, bu[t] like I said, they had been doing this for a long time: coaches, special outfits, hairdos, makeup. We were there with regular Sunday clothes and a suit with no training— nothing—*talk about a long shot!*

There were several different areas of the competition: modeling, talent etc. For one part of the competition Anthony had to create a short commercial. I thought we just weren't prepared. The other kids were like robots, trained to move, smile, turn, etc., typical pageant stuff. Well, these kids were no match for the natural charisma and talent he had. He shined like a diamond in the sand!

It was fun, and he did win first place. The really funny thing, however, was afterwards when I thought about it, I realized how I thought the odds were so against him, but Anthony never once felt like he was in over his head; he gave it 110%, enjoyed every moment of it, and took the most out of that day that he could. It was actually Anthony who had the upper hand because you can't teach or coach someone to have that kind of personality and charisma. It was just natural for him.

This is Anthony in everything he does. He does everything 110% and with heart! He has certainly had his challenges, his dark moments, but he not only pushed through them, he learned and became a better person.

They say some people are watchers, some are doers—Anthony is a doer. He has a huge heart; he likes to see people happy; he wants to be involved; people interest him; things interest him; he truly loves life; and nothing and nobody can ever diminish his zest for life!

—Sue Tauro

***

There was no way I could tell this story of Aunt Sue, my godmother, and her dream of getting me involved in modelling and perhaps Hollywood?—any better than in Aunt Sue's own, genuine words. Her testimonial memory of my first "male modeling/kid" competition brings a twinkle to my eye even now. It really was fun! I just had to win the contest, and I was used to winning with hockey.

I was just a kid, only eleven, but it made such an impression on me. In some odd sense of accomplishment, it seemed to go hand-in-hand with hockey. *I was the star; I was the one the audience had come to see; I had to live up to my reputation on the ice or in a silly costume and a hand-me-down suit from one of my cousins.*

Two years later, I was still competing at 13 years old, and had won two more competitions. So, what started out as a lark, a joke, to keep my mind distracted, became us going to the state competition. This was strictly Aunt Sue's project. My parents didn't understand modeling, especially male kids' modeling, any more than they did hockey, but at least with hockey they were used to its ups-and-downs.

You're going to laugh, but my "talent" costume was *"Mickey Mouse"*! I don't know if it was just easy to obtain or if we just happened to have one in the house somewhere. Luckily, I was just cocky enough to pull it off. I had the *worst 80s-band hairdo as well,* courtesy of Aunt Sue's unusual sense of style and humor. Anyway, it worked. I won!

This brainstorm by my god-mother would help me in the future when there didn't seem to be anywhere else to go, but at one point I would fight it tooth-and-nail. Ask anybody in my family—I just never followed the rules.

Chapter Twenty: Exodus of Family to Up State NY, *"I had to go too?"*

Not sure how we all made it, but "made it" we did. This is a picture of the three Williams children. Me before I got sick; Michelle, my oldest sister, blonde; and Tara, darker. We were so happy in this picture. Tara was the first in the family to decide to move to Up State New York with her husband Daryl. This is how it all happened.

Tara and her husband Daryl moved to Dutchess County, New York, quite some time before "9-11" became a household terror. During this time their marriage seemed solid, but the family dynamic went through so many changes during this timeframe that many good things, unfortunately, fell by the wayside. One of them being Tara and Daryl's marriage. Tara and I were closest in age, and we talked bout these things before I started college. Was she happy in her marriage? It seemed so, but since I was the younger, baby brother, I always heard everything last. Yet, it didn't bother me. I was still, at this time, all wrapped up in hockey. I believed so firmly in my heart that I was going to find a way to make it happen. But as you know, I wasn't able to hold it together.

Michelle, on the other hand, the next to move up to Dutchess County, went through a trauma that affected each and every one of us. Michelle's husband Gabby and father to her two children, Elizabeth and Gabby, Jr., was still commuting an hour each way back and forth to New York for his job. Gabby, Jr., was just 6 months old. I wasn't as involved in this tragedy as much as the rest of the family because I was away at college, getting into trouble and relishing all the freedom that made me take my eyes off the course of my own life.

"Looking back, it kind of seems like things were falling apart for the whole family; well, I I guess in many ways, they were ... for all of us. We just didn't know it at the time; nor could we ever have imagined the numbing shock that was just around the corner for every American family."

My parent's move to Dutchess County, New York, had been planned for some time. They were going to sell the house in New Rochelle when I started college and move up to be with their daughters, son-in-laws, and grandchildren. It made sense, even though I just sort of ignored it all.

The trip for Gabby to work, however, was extended even more when Michelle and he moved closer to the rest of the family, but it seemed like a good trade-off with the new baby, and he was able to be with the family in a home, rather than a small apartment. Like all of middle-class America, everyone was struggling to raise their families and live the American dream.

One morning on the way to work, Gabby found himself in dire circumstances. The roads were slick, and darkness loomed over the highway. He was reaching for his phone so it wouldn't get wedged between the seats just as his eyes were adjusting to the dim surroundings. *Did he see his life flash before his eyes?* Maybe, we really don't know.

He barely saw the deer crossing the road in front of his car, but he instinctively swerved out of the way. This swift action on wet, icy roads derailed Gabby's car into the guardrail, flipping the car end-over-end. When the Authorities arrived, Gabby had to be cut out of the car, while an airlift was called to med-evac him to the nearest hospital. The airlift arrived but had to wait. Getting him out of the twisted vehicle took considerable time.

After rushing Gabby to the hospital, it was learned that he had lost all sensation from the waist down. There was no time for the family to accept all this or to adjust to the repercussions that would be entailed in his care. There were no "what-ifs" to talk about; there was only preparations and accommodations. The whole family came together to be supportive and helpful. It was what we always did for each other.

I remember sitting with Michelle as she completely broke down. She didn't know what the next move would be or how she was going to keep her family together. Michelle had always been the strong one who kept me calm when things were touch-and-go with all my issues. Now it was my turn to *step up to the plate* and be the big brother.

In their darkest of times, both of my sisters came to me for my opinion and extra hugs. They knew I would always listen, and they would get understanding and encouragement, but straight talk as well because even more solemn events would affect my family as Tara and Daryl's marriage fell apart; Gabby was cared for and later left the family; endocarditis was not that far in my future. We've almost come full circle here, with "my step back in time". I just have a little bit more to share.

Caring for other people and providing advice to my friends and family has always been something which makes me feel good. It provides me with a sense of empowerment, especially when I was weak, sick, out of control, depressed, or as you will soon see … lost in addiction. Each of these upcoming events rocked the family in different ways, but we always stuck together no matter the enormity of the circumstances. *"My support system, it was definitely the best to be had. It was a shame I didn't listen more."*

As I mentioned before, when I bombed out of college and out of hockey, this was the only place left for me to go: the town of Wappingers, Dutchess County, New York, to be with my family.

Chapter Twenty-one: After 9-11, *"How did my family react? And me?"*

September 11, 2001, affected all of us, but in very different ways. Being a New Yorker, I had friends with family members that were close to or inside the towers. My family knew hundreds, if not thousands, of people, friends, acquaintances, co-workers, classmates, on and on, that were affected, but we all did. We were all Americans.

One of my uncles was in an armored car that day, picking up money drops in New York from large companies. You know the type of vehicle—one was attacked and idolized on-screen in the movie "Heat". *That's one you don't soon forget!*

We all remember where we were that morning and exactly what we were doing. I was no exception. It may have taken me a little longer to react, *but I got there.*

I was so self-absorbed in the devastation of my own life that it just didn' register with me that anything out of the ordinary was going on until a frienc contacted me who was panicking because he couldn't find a family member. turned on the television, only to see people jumping out of windows and anothe plane hitting the second tower. I just stood there, my mouth dropping open in disbelief.

It looked like a dramatized movie to me. *Was this the old story about "The War of the Worlds" radio broadcast coming true? This just couldn't be real!*

It was in this surreal moment that my own phone rang, and I was notified that my Uncle Mark was *"AT THE TOWERS!"* The chain reaction of family calls was going out, but it took a little time for the information to catch up to us all that Uncle Mark had already left The Twin Towers before they were hit. Did he feel guilty afterwards; after the relief wore off? Who knows? You just don't talk about stuff like that.

Yet, the information was so sketchy and phone service so limited, we still wondered for quite some time whether it was accurate or not. Everything was "...unsure, not verified, not validated; presumed..." **Everything was in-limbo! With no real answers!**

I finally received the news that Uncle Mark was safe—he was okay—but what about all the other people, all the other New Yorkers, who weren't *"...okay; couldn't be accounted for; were already dead or dying or suffering or...?"* It was *just too ghastly to be true!*

In reflection, I saw only one positive emotion that came out of all of this. New Yorkers," like me and my family, along with every other single person in the great nation of ours were united as we have never been before or since in the fight against terrorism. War had come to the United States of America, and *we were united!*

***

Yet, through it all, there were other doubts as well. I remember not being able to shake the feeling of uncertainty that it was actually going on ... in real time. Some of us didn't even think about conspiracy at first. *Was it an accident? Air Traffic Controller botch-job? So many unanswered questions ... at first!*

Although, we did initially feel a sense of unease and vulnerability. I mean, stuff like this wasn't supposed to happen in the U.S. Not here, on American soil ... this was the terrorism of foreign countries, the Middle East, not ours!

Even though this wasn't a common occurrence, it still felt like things were never going to be the same again. Things were going to change forever. And they did!

On that day, 9-11-01, we wouldn't have the terrorist theory verified until The Pentagon, in Virginia right outside of Washington, D.C., was destroyed by another plane, brought down by brave Americans willing to sacrifice their lives to stop the terrorism in the skies over our red-white-and-blue country ... the land of the free.

My family remained, however, as it always had, totally stalwart and unified. Little did we know that our own family towers were getting ready to tumble down as well. Through all of this to come, my family stayed tight, supportive, and loving. It hadn't changed since the day I was born and hasn't changed now. And it never will. I know that about my family. We've stood hand-in-hand, taking our beatings when we had to, always together. Each time that we rose from the ashes like a Phoenix, we shined ever brighter.

***

About a year after this horrific, mindset-altering event, my own life took another turn no one expected, least of all me. This was my time to crumble, and again, it affected my entire family. *Why does someone so young have to experience yet "another" crisis with no chance to recover?*

There are always questions to which there are no answers, no "whys?" Advice is given freely, but answers have to be earned through truth, acceptance, revelation, and digging deeper within yourself than you ever thought possible. I won't say this was easy for me because it wasn't. I had my own blocks to break through. Blocks I had been cultivating since I was a baby.

These are my experiences from my earliest memories. Yet, with my secretive nature, it left me personally feeling alone, afraid, and confused. Navigating through this from such an early age, however, allowed me to see other people's problems and traumatic events. I might not have been able to fix my own situations, but since I could see these things happening to friends and even strangers all around me, maybe I could be of assistance. It was really upsetting, though, to be able to put a smile on someone else's face that was genuine when I knew my smile was but the face of the clown, hiding my tears beneath makeup and shrill laughter.

Talk about feeling like a prisoner? I was locked in a cage of my own design because I thought it would be fun, a lark like modeling and coming up with my own costumes and creative monologues coached by Aunt Sue, that would allow me to experiment with any and everything I wanted to conquer. After all, I always won the modeling competitions; I was sought after as a hockey player.

"Only to have it all blow up in my face again, and really, in reflection, it hasn't stopped yet."

I'm still living and giving and bouncing off the walls. My family unit is intact. I bring you back now to "the rest of the story." So, take a deep breath, and I'll tell you where it all went from here to more chaos, upheaval, fear, and pain. I believe that love makes the difference, and that's why I'm still here, writing my memoir to help others like myself because I know you're out there.

"I'm writing this for you!"

My Family, Thanksgiving Day, 2018

Me, in front, being the clown, as always…

Mom and Dad; Kendyl, my wife

And our two beautiful children = LOVE!

SECTION VI

The Illness That Changed Everything

"This begins the rest of my story. There's lots more

to come!"

Chapter Twenty-two: Where Were We? *"What was I doing here?"*

Wappingers, New York, was the little town where my family settled in Dutchess County, Upstate New York. To say that I was out of my element would be an understatement. The most recent population census for this small borough is 5,522, based on 2010 statistics. *Believe me, it was a whole lot less when we relocated in 2001!*

We went from being just 20 minutes out of Manhattan to a place named for the Algonquian Nation of Native Americans, dating back to the mid-17th century, who resided on the eastern side of Wappingers Creek. This creek flowed into the Hudson River. The Indian word for a cascade or waterfall of rushing water over the rocks and inclines of Up State New York is "Wappinger".

Two small communities are separated by *"the creek"*: Wappingers, of course, and Poughkeepsie on the western side of the creek. This slice of water through the countryside can be raging, especially with the snowfall thaw in the early spring, or trickling if we have a hot, rainless summer. The trickle doesn't happen often. Wet weather drifts down from Canada, across the Hudson, and flows to all its tributaries.

"So, for this city boy from just outside New York City, it was like the end of the earth for me. It could be peaceful and quiet, which was what my family for looking for ... for retirement and raising a family, but this was the time of my life when I was looking for fun, frolic, action, career, and a future. None of which I had going for me. And remember, no backup plan, either."

I also felt like I had lost everything when I left the University, settling for Dutchess Community College, since I had lost my dream and my chance at playing for the New York Rangers. *They certainly weren't going to find me up here in this backwoods town!*

*"I didn't know who I was anymore, but I **did** know that community college wasn't going to fix anything."* Did this become a self-fulling prophecy? Was I angry and lashing out without really trying?

Yeah, I guess I was. I was being a selfish brat who couldn't admit I had brought it all down upon myself. But, believe me, getting sick again wasn't the answer!

How could I be sick again? Endocarditis! How long had the Cardiologist been warning us about this? In my happy-go-lucky-*seeming* way, where I hide all the important stuff from myself and everybody else, I just didn't think about these things. I never, ever believed it could really happen.

***

This is where my story actually began in Chapter One, when I had the Revelation, *"What if there is no tomorrow?"*

Well, by now, my reader knows there was a tomorrow. After all, I'm writing this and sharing my experiences in the hopes that you won't have to face some of the rude awakenings I lived through and am still living with on a daily basis.

Yeah, I continued to hide things from myself and everyone else too. *"Some things never change."* But by buckling down and putting these words together in logical order, I'm seeing and realizing so many things I never saw before. Not while I was living it; not while I was shying away from the bare, hard-cold facts.

Facts are indisputable, so it is said. Well, maybe they are and maybe they aren't. *Perception of the facts can alter even the most analytical among us.*

I've been hiding a BIG fact from my readers since the first draft of this book. I worked so hard, up late at night while I worked all day, putting together what I called "my vomited-up life story" in rapid spurts and stops and rethinking and rewriting and just continuing to add, add, add to it to get everything in there. Now, it's being torn apart and rewritten with some clarity, cohesiveness, and accuracy with things in order pretty much, so to speak. Quite a task!

Now I have more time to devote to this project, and devoted I am! Somewhere in the early transitions of *this* draft, the company I worked for shut its doors, unexpectedly. So, I've been job hunting too. I have a family to feed. I'm looking for just the right thing and am very encouraged, but it has been a long haul emotionally and financially to get to the point of being able to write and promote this Self-Help Memoir.

… So, back to the rest of the story with another pressure to overcome.

"Yet, I know I'll do it! And take everyone reading right along with me as I find out just where I need to be in life. Everyone has a place. We all just have to find it."

Chapter Twenty-three: Back to the Beginning,

"Tomorrow came..."

The rest of my family seemed happy living in the much quieter atmosphere of Up State New York. Me, on the other hand, had been forced into this move with nowhere else to go, no plan for the future, and definitely no backup plan if things didn't work out; which of course, nothing ever work outs exactly the way we envision it in our dreams.

In my case, however, I felt like I had been denied everything. I was angry, hurt, disillusioned, and in self-destruct mode by losing my dream of playing professional hockey. Absolutely nothing else interested me except my own self-pity, self-criticism, and total absence of self-esteem. This, unfortunately, led to a complete lack of control on my part. Even worse than it had been at the University where I at least had a great time slacking off and getting into trouble. Nothing was fun after 9-11. I had far too much time on my hands and a chip on my shoulder that exposed me to far too many negative influences.

On top of that, I was trying to get my bearings in a whole new environment, navigating uncharted waters. I had no friends; I'd forfeited the one shot I had at following up on the good education I'd received at Iona Prep School; and I self-sabotaged myself at Dutchess County Community College, dropping out after only one year. It was a self-fulfilling prophecy that a small college couldn't me get back on track again. My mom wasn't happy about it, but like everything else she'd suggested to me, she took it in stride. She always was and still is my guiding angel. Even when she was pretty much fed up with me and my shenanigans, she didn't let it show.

I started taking part-time jobs, small-town employment with no future, and piece-meal projects, but I did manage to make some friends. Somewhere along the way, more remote family members moved closer to us and one of the daughters worked in a real-estate office. The idea of becoming a real-estate tycoon stuck in my brain—it sounded easy enough—even though I knew relatively nothing about it. I mean, I remembered when my parents put their house on the market in New Rochelle. It seemed like something I could do using my charm and personality which Aunt Sue had made such a big fuss over when I was doing the modeling competition. After all, I won those. This could work!

After a few questions were answered by those who knew me, family and friends, I had a direction to follow. This was a big step for me. I was believing in something else besides sports and hockey for the first time in my life.

I took the required courses and studied for the test to get my license. I had to drive two hours to Albany, New York, to take the exam. And with my luck, of course, I failed it. *So, what did I do?* I did what I always do—I called my mom.

told her I didn't pass the test, and I should just give up … little did she know how much I wanted to *"give up"* on everything, even on life itself.

I did tell mom that I'd found out that the test was being given again that same afternoon. Mom gave me a pep talk that I still remember to this day. She told me giving up wasn't an option. After all, I had really been nervous when I'd left home to go to Albany, and all the time I had to think about it on the long drive there only added to my apprehension. She assured me that I would pass the test on the retake. Somehow this broken person that I had become hung onto to those words of encouragement.

I didn't have any money to go anywhere or do anything, so I had to just sit in my car for the next few hours. I tried not to think about the test and obsess over the outcome. I kept listening to my mom's encouragement over and over.

I was much more comfortable taking the test a second time, and finally with a passing grade, I could finally smile again. I guess I hadn't realized how fragile I really was at this time. It was quite an awakening, a frightening jolt! It felt so unnatural for me to lack confidence when I'd always had it in such abundance, but this wasn't hockey; this was my life!

This was the tomorrow in which I had to find my own way to becoming a full, functional adult. This is what I needed to reunite with my strong, loving family.

Chapter Twenty-four: Endocarditis Take Two: *"How do survive?"*

Well, it may seem like we've come full circle back to the beginning of the book, but there was a lot more going on with the treatment, seclusion, pain, and helplessness of endocarditis than what was written in Chapter One. There's so much I didn't share upfront because it was just too much for me to think about and may have been overwhelming for my readers, the very people I hope I can help by sharing my own shortcomings.

Even though I was trying to make a future in the Real Estate business, I was being influenced by a new group of friends who were more interested in staying up all night—*Beer Pong and Mario Parties*—with plenty of cutting up, gags, laughs, flirtations, and everything in excess. Perfect environment for the class clown, now all grown up, or at least I thought I was grown up.

Unlike before, however, the endocarditis was ***not*** caused by the bad decisions I made after my chance to play pro-hockey for the New York Rangers became a dream that was never to be. Sure, bitterness remained, and I was continuing to hide my true feelings on just about everything from everyone, including my very loving, supportive family. Selfishly, I wasn't even thinking about my family. I had wandered into a surreal environment that helped me to cope, but certainly didn't help me to mature. My mom and dad, sisters and their husbands, just let me do my own thing. I wasn't in any hurry to tell them the shallowness of my existence, but of course, they already knew. News and reputations travel fast in a small community like Wappingers.

This was a catastrophic event like a semi with busted breaks charging down a steep hill, destroying everything in its path that couldn't get out of the way fast enough as the momentum escalated, and the driver lost total control. I was holding on for dear life, but would my strong, stubborn willpower be enough to get me through this ordeal and all its repercussions unscathed? The answer to this question, for the first time, was an absolute, *"No."*

There was only so much friends and family could do to help me through this sickness and marginal recovery anyway, but I certainly wasn't going to ask for help either. *"No, not yet. Perhaps that would come later since tomorrow continued to come as regularly as the dawn."*

***

After my grueling stay in the hospital, only to return home to the same basic routine with a visiting nurse and my mother's diligent care, even though she couldn't hide her worry and tiredness from me, I was far from being a model patient. I never once thought about how Mom must really feel, what she was really thinking. After all, she'd seen me in distress before, but this was the first time she ever questioned whether I would make it through this infection or not. And, it was only going to get worse.

In fact, I was harder to get along with at home than I ever was in the hospital. This was my family. I could yell at them and complain to them and be a real jerk. They understood what I was going through, right? So, I didn't have to try and pretty it up for them. Even my friends and other family members who came to visit me at home to try and make the total bedrest time go quicker, didn't seem to help me in the least. I was just plain angry. It wasn't right; it wasn't fair!

It was Dad in his nightly seemingly inconsequential talks with me where I finally noticed the concern in his eyes and the fear, but behind that fear I could feel him asking me to keep on fighting. My parents weren't giving up on me, so I realized I couldn't give up on them. It calmed some of the anger but replaced it with the same fear they were trying so desperately to hide. So, from outbursts to quiet solitude. I never knew which mood was going to surface; either did they. It was like a time bomb ticking off the seconds of my life.

I had no answers for anyone, family or friends, when they tried to get me to talk about this ordeal. All I could do is go through the motions, do what I was told, try to stay positive, but optimism and being the jokester was losing its charm, even on me. My copying mechanism was crumbling to dust.

"How was I supposed to survive this time, when no one seemed to have any answers?"

Chapter Twenty-five: Good News; Bad News, *"Why always bad, too?"*

I could say it's the story of my life, but it's true with everybody—*you have to take the bad with the good. I guess it's supposed to even out that way. Who knows? It's in everyone's life.*

I received the news, even though I really didn't feel much different, that the infection was receding somewhat. I do remember that sudden burst of, *"Yes, I'm winning!"* Yet, there was something changing inside of me; I could feel it. I was hesitant, afraid to feel good about anything because I knew, I guess intuitively, that I'd just get knocked down and kicked in the teeth. This was my dream of playing hockey being crushed all over again.

All of my heretofore perceptions and perspective about the future were altering. Was I really growing up this time? I remained positive, but I kept waiting for *the other shoe to fall.* It was engrained in me to look at the other side of things, the hidden possibilities that no one was talking about. At least, not yet. I was always anticipating the worst possible scenario because that seemed to be all that ever happened for me.

I became a master at projecting good news for everyone else and hiding how scared I really was deep inside of me. Easy for me to do; I'd been doing that since was a kid. It was all a self-defense mechanism to protect me from showing how vulnerable and subject to failure I really was. But I did wonder, *"Why now? When the news was encouraging..."*

So even when the blood tests came back that the infection had totally cleared up, the next step was an even bigger tragedy. It was time to discuss open-heart surgery.

***

These discussions had started with my parents and the cardiologist weeks/months earlier, back when I was in the hospital, as early as New Year's Day in the ER. They didn't hide this from me, but maybe I just couldn't look that far ahead or perhaps I thought if the infection was gone ...well, I wouldn't need this risky surgery. The fact was evident from the start, however, that saving my heart in its current state was impossible.

I must have realized this, but I didn't want to think about it, so I didn't. The decision had been made over six weeks earlier that an artificial heart valve was the best way to go, *if needed.* Yeah, those two little words, *"if needed,"* allowed me to hope it wouldn't be needed.

Everyone but me already had accepted that... *"It was needed. No ifs, ands, or buts..."* Even my sisters, Michelle and Tara knew; my brothers-in-law knew. I should have known, but it was just too much for me to grasp at 21 years old with my whole life in front of me. *Well, maybe it was or maybe it wasn't.*

The six weeks of bed rest gave me way too much time to think. I had always been a remarkably healthy guy with a heart murmur that the doctor had to keep an eye on. I was an athlete, very physical and strong in every way. *This wasn't supposed to happen!*

Even though I was hiding the truth from myself and everyone around once again, I knew deep in my heart *(Ha, ha...great pun, right?)* that I had to switch gears. I needed to rely on my brain because my body was failing. *Ya' just can't live without a heart.*

This was the first time I had to come face-to-face with the fact that this was much more than just another hurdle to overcome. This was not life-altering or life-shortening; this could be life-ending. Wow, it was really a tough *"what if?"* to wrap my thoughts around. I'd been so busy waiting for life to begin that I had never considered that it had begun 21 years earlier, when I was born with a condition that wouldn't allow me to take nourishment into my body. They found the heart murmur that prevented me from playing sports, specifically hockey, when I was only two years old.

All I had to do was look in the mirror to see that it was true. I'd lost a bunch of weight, and as a hockey player and not a big guy to start with, I certainly didn't need to lose any weight. My skin was grayish in color; my eyes were glassy yet flat-looking. My smile didn't light up my face anymore. I looked like an old man in a young man's body. I was wasting away to nothing, and I had no energy. I could barely breathe. I was so tired all the time.

I knew then, if I hadn't known it before, that I would never skate again. I would never play hockey even with the other guys in the family or from my old neighborhood.

"Why is the bad news always so much worse than the brief high the good news allows one to feel for just a few moments in the grand scheme of things?

The next section tells how it felt for me".

SECTION VII

After the Bacterial Infection, Endocarditis

"Was my worst nightmare coming true? YES!"

Chapter Twenty-six: Heart Valve, *"OMG, what about my family?"*

Each week my blood was tested, and *"we"—my immediate family and I; Mom, Dad, Michelle, Tara, and me*—were given an immediate update. So far, the results were encouraging. The disease endocarditis was showing up less in the bloodstream, which proved that my body was fighting the disease and holding its own, gradually getting stronger as the endocarditis became less and less in the percentages revealed by my white-blood cell count getting lower when it attacked the infection with fewer cells as the disease was brought under control, and the healthy red-blood cells were more plentiful. *Yes! I was getting healthy again! I really was winning!*

Yet, the condition of my heart could not be changed, as I had so hoped a miracle would occur to make it heal itself as "I" healed. *"Yeah, I know, we'd all been told that was impossible, but I felt like I'd done the impossible before. Why not now?"*

I wonder looking back, and of course there's no way of knowing, but did my parents and sisters have the same unrealistic faith in me that I had? I think that they probably did because it was obvious that we were all suffering, and some of my family may even have been starting to give up hope. I could see it in my mother's and sisters' swollen eyes and hear it in the deathly silence of space that used to be filled with my father's strong voice. We were all tired and about at the end of our ropes. Each blood test gave a little spark of relief, only to be followed by the inevitable.

There's a big difference between "improbable" and "impossible," with "improbable" relating back to those two words I clung to in the last chapter, *"if needed"*; and "impossible" being finite, absolute: *"No going back; no crossing GO and collecting $200.00 like in the game of Monopoly."* So, it was all just a matter of time before another opportunistic infection or "bug" came along that would create another crisis which my heart could never withstand.

"Without open-heart surgery and a new mechanical valve, I was going to be just another *'Goner'*—*unfortunately, sooner rather than later.*"

***

Everything was being handled by my cardiologist, someone I knew and who knew me. She had called in an Internal Medicine Specialist as soon as the bacterial infection was found on that fateful New Year's Day in 2004. Between the two of them, my treatment was set up with a Picc-line inserted directly into my heart before I ever left the ER and was admitted into the hospital for a week long of painful blood testing every half-hour and constant monitoring while connected to a big machine which administered a heavy-duty drug that *"could"* cause permanent loss f my hearing and/or eyesight. It was scary, but it was also the only thing that could e done.

This bulky machine became a permanent fixture in my bedroom when I ame home. The treatment continued just as it had in-patient, with the same uncertain prognosis, progress reports, weekly blood tests, and an in-home nurse to help my mom with the specialized care. I knew Mom was watching me and working o make things easier for me *"around the clock"*. She stayed with me practically all the time, with just short breaks when Dad would see me every night after work or one of my sisters came over. Friends and other family came by too, but I was getting too frail to be much of a clown for them. The weakness was overwhelming, and I kept thinking about what I had to look forward to … nothing really. I didn't even think about real estate anymore.

With the infection finally cleared from my bloodstream, a surgeon was selected by the cardiologist and brought into the mix. The discussion about artificial valve versus valve transplant was initiated again, but it was more like common courtesy or procedural rhetoric because the choice had already been made; the pros-and-cons analyzed and weighed in every possible manner.

After meeting with the Internal Medicine Specialist around Week 5, I guess, I was starting to feel a little bit of hope. I was moving forward and that was so much better than total bedrest and no progress at all!

Everyday presented its own challenges in survival tactics, and when I was wasn't in pain or confused by trying to process all the repercussions from this infection, I would sleep often, but only for short periods of time. Back then, I didn't realize that my parents were terrified each time I went to sleep that I would never wake up. I guess that's when my folks talked about things together. That must have been when my mother cried.

With two beautiful youngsters of my own now, I can't even begin to fathom how they must have felt. Even though death is a constant companion in everyone's life, it just doesn't seem fair for parents to be forced into constant deathwatch with their own child. The law of the land is that each generation will outlive the ones before. I really don't know how my family withstood all this. I can only shake my head and marvel at their strength and fortitude.

I was so lucky to have the visiting nurse that was assigned to my case. It did give my parents a much-needed break, and even though I wasn't the most pleasant patient she could have asked for, we make a truce that lasted for the duration as she extended her visits to talk, but mostly to laugh and joke with me. She helped the whole family accept the situation as well as was humanly possible. She went the extra mile for me and my family, and I am eternally grateful.

It was a rough six weeks of bedrest for all involved with a recalcitrant 21-year old *"baby"*. Afterall, I was the youngest in the family, and the only son.

"Time creeped along in elongated seconds with boredom in every moment, but my family must have felt each second was precious and relished each one as if it might be my last!"

Chapter Twenty-seven: Giving Me My Life Back, *"What life?"*

Things switched into upper gear almost unexpectedly. It had been such boredom—seeded with pain, fear, unknowing, and confusion—for so long that when Dr. Argenzianno was the man tasked with *"giving me my life back"*, everybody knew it wouldn't be the same old Anthony, jokester and would-be Real Estate Tycoon. All my dreams had come to a halt!

Once all the clearances were given, I was going directly into surgery with *another* six-plus weeks of recovery time, giving us no time to think about it, react to it, and plan for the uncertain future. We were a family set adrift in a turbulent sea with all kinds of problems facing us at every turn. As I mentioned, there was more drama underneath the surface of things, especially with Gabby's tragic, permanent condition and Tara's uncertain marriage, which I knew very little about. Everything relating to the family at this time was deliberately kept from me. I was to concentrate on getting better.

We had to drive down to Columbia Presbyterian Hospital in New York City. It was a very emotional and draining trip. This would be the first time I personally met Dr. Argenzianno. I was nervous and so was everybody else.

I had already been told that I was the youngest person *ever* to have mechanical valve replacement done by robotic means. I actually thought for a brief second that it was kind of cool, but all I had to do is look at my parents' faces to know that their nerves were just about shot.

Putting up with me has never been easy, but now? It was impossible. And Mom and Dad had been discussing and agonizing over this all the time I was fighting the endocarditis, never once mentioning it to me. They let me hope, just in case another option presented itself, but of course, they already knew that wasn't going to happen. *"If needed"* was never a part of the equation.

I knew this was the very moment upon which my whole life and future, if there was one, was hinged. My parents had been taking care of me, working to keep the family going, and struggling to process everything that would keep our lives together … as a unit, as a family, as the united team we had always been.

The strain was so thick in the car you could feel it. We were all holding on for dear life, literally, just waiting for the verdict to be handed down. No one had really told me the chances of the operation failing and what that meant or what it meant to die on the table, but those thoughts niggled me all the way from Dutchess County, Upper State New York, to the big city near where we used to live. I certainly didn't feel like coming home, but then again, New York City was still a cesspool of devastation from the terrorist attack.

***

The meeting went as expected, especially for my parents who had heard it all before, and they had been really honest with me about the medical procedure and recuperation. The surgery was imminent and would be rather immediate. After all, all the reports on my blood work and x-rays, preliminary examination, etc., had been done when I was in the hospital 6 weeks prior. Then the doctor said something that caught my attention and upset me greatly.

Dr. Argenzianno began to explain about the cost of this new procedural, robotics surgery. He talked about insurance, other options, what was covered, what may not be totally covered, and the gist was that it was going to be a very costly operation. I wanted to stop the conversation right then and there by screaming, "My father has worked hard all his life!" I couldn't believe that he was going to jeopardize all their savings, when he was so near retirement, to do this for me. *"My folks were going to lose everything because of me! Was I worth it? There wasn't even any guarantee that I would survive the surgery! What then? They still had to pay for it!"*

As tears of love filled my eyes in the shadow of my mother just barely holding it together, and my father subdued as I have never seen him before, I was ready to bail out and scream... "STOP!"

Chapter Twenty-eight, The Surgeon, *"Could he really stop this?"*

Looking back now, I don't know how much should have been attributed to fear or whether I really did feel unworthy of the family I had been blessed with. *Probably, a little of both.*

I do know that in my own psyche I was emotionally drained, fed-up, just sick to death of it all! *(Ha, ha ... great pun! Famous last words...)* I had never contemplated "death" before; I knew the endocarditis was serious and the side effects of the drugs could be life-altering—perhaps losing my hearing or sight—but this experimental robotic surgery on someone my age could be "life-ending". Mom and Dad, even Michelle and Tara, skirted this issue around me, and of course, I wouldn't talk to anyone about it, either. Chock it up to another secret I kept carefully guarded. They were really starting to pile up!

My extreme reaction at a desperate time about money and what this would do to my folks was legitimate, but I also knew it affected the whole family, even my nieces and nephews. We all relied on each other, and *now with one operation, I was gonna' blow it for everyone!*

This *"mental gymnastics"* which flooded my mind showed that I had total understanding of everything involved. Yeah, desperate is the right word to describe my guilt, my shame, my inadequacies, my liabilities, and my uselessness. I was getting emotional over every little thing because no matter how positive the force conversations with my family *seemed to be,* there was still a distinct chance that it all could go horribly wrong. And hey! This is me we're talking about. I hadn't exactly conquered everything that had been thrown in my life's journey to this point. *I couldn't even play hockey anymore, and this cinched that fact that I never would again ... not even in mock-play with my cousins. I would never be able to get on the ice again...*

***

I will never forget how my temper peaked when I met Dr. Argenzianno, the one person who could help me. The meeting that first day ended on a better note, however, when the surgeon turned to me like he was noticing me for the first time and said, "I don't care how much this costs; I am going to perform the surgery and fix you!"

My parents, who had such worried faces just moments before, almost smiled and looked relieved. We could deal with the monetary aspect after the fact. The highest priority was making me whole again; at least as whole as I can ever be with a mechanical valve, which if you remember from earlier in the book developed a slight leak right after I started working on this manuscript. Let's hope when I return for my yearly physical later this year that it hasn't gotten any worse.

My emotional outbursts had begun quite some time before this fated meeting with the doctor. Everyone in the family could see it happening to me as I got scared, then angry, then solemn and quiet, even uncooperative. I really have no idea how they put up with me so calmly when I was sarcastic and morbid, unreasonable and moody.

Even my sisters' children were wary of me. I noticed their big eyes as they took in the big machine in my bedroom, which they didn't really understand was keeping me alive. I tried to laugh and joke with them, but I wasn't in a joking mood. My ever-ready humor was evaporating. I was an emotional wreck and processing the upcoming surgery was like raging at a raw, jagged wound which would never heal and would continue to fester, bleed, drain, and deplete me until nothing was left.

I was the youngest of my family, but *"the kids"* really brought it home to me that another generation was forming in front of us. *Maybe I would be the first in the family to become obsolete?* It really didn't seem fair! And yes, then the tears would come, but only in the dark of night when everyone thought I was asleep. I was completely falling apart! We all were!

Dr. Argenzianno gave me the most precious gift I've ever received, even before he scrubbed in and asked for that first scalpel. His confidence gave me hope, which previously I hadn't been able to accept. And I could see that same quiet hope filling the tired eyes of my parents and easing their fears which they'd managed to keep from me during the 6 weeks of treatment for the bacterial infection.

We were back together again as we had always been, locked in a common bond that transcended all time and space. The tears that coursed down my cheeks went from angry resentment to happy acceptance in a flash. I didn't know what my life was going to be like after this surgery, but for the first time I believed I wouldn't "die on the table". I just couldn't do that to my family. They needed me as much as I needed them.

"One small word, one huge step forward...HOPE!"

Chapter Twenty-nine: Gearing Up for the Fight of My Life, *"Love!"*

We had to go through the logistics and education for the surgery. We set a date for the robotic operation, and I was given videos to watch so that I could understand what was going to happen to me. These showed exactly what would be taking place. My parents and sisters, the whole family even my brothers-in-law—everyone except the children, of course—watched these with me. I would sometimes watch them again late at night after everyone was sleeping. I would turn the sound off and just concentrate on every single detail that was occurring. I figured the more I knew, the better it would be. *I don't know if it made any difference or not, but I felt like I was doing something to help the process, the surgery, and most importantly, my recuperation.*

There is no way to define "pain" and "helplessness" in this type of situation. The videos were accurate, but sterile in a sense; we didn't see the suffering. We couldn't feel the emotion of the patients who slept peacefully through the operation. I couldn't quite grasp the concept of the emotional, mental, and physical pain that I would have to endure. *And of course, I thought I'd been through so much already that this couldn't be any worse. I was wrong...*

***

There was so much planning to be done by everyone in the family. This was a change in my life, in my whole family's lives, that seemed surreal at the time. Everything revolved around what was going to happen when I came home from the hospital. Everyone would have to adjust to my post-surgery accommodations. Even the kids had to be talked to about keeping the noise down, how I was going to be tired and fragile, and how they could help by being good boys and girls. These conversations took place mostly without me, but kids being kids, they would come look at me with wary eyes and anticipation. They didn't really understand, but they could feel the undercurrents in my parents' home where I resided. Thankfully, the whole family was together.

My world was revolving around me, but not in any way I could ever have expected or hoped for. This was a stardom I had never wanted when I had been playing at being a model with my Godmother Sue. This was not the type of celebrity I had wanted to become even as a hockey professional. I could feel the fear in the air as if it were in the very air I breathed.

This time getting sick was the beginning of a long process which would change me forever. I knew these things. Everyone in the family did, but we went through the motions like everything was okay; everything was normal; all the pain and suffering was going to end; I was going to be the same young adult I had been before this all happened. *Fat chance!*

All I can say at this juncture is that we were all living on dreams, hope, and Love... We were also exhausted and not fooling anyone. The tension was so thick you could cut it with a knife. My mom and dad were withdrawn and fearful, even as they put on encouraging faces for me. The fact remains that we all knew I was living *"On Borrowed Time..."*

This is where my story truly begins. The first 21 years had been a dress rehearsal.

This was the real deal. This was the point of no return.

Chapter Thirty: The First Time My Life Changed Forever

"Why?"

As readers, you have shared with me my story filled with success and failure, broken dreams, and optimistic enthusiasm. Yet this operation, this robotic surgery, would change all aspects of my life, even my friendships and life-long plans which were half-baked anyway, but this certainly wasn't the path I had ever thought I would end up on.

I was a fighter; I was a winner! *Why was this happening to me? I was only 21 years old. Life was supposed to be just beginning. All I could think about was that it was ending. Even if I lived, there would be restrictions and fears dominating my future. This mechanical heart valve would dictate what I could and could not do for the rest of my life.*

Also, there were some immediate complications that were a little surprising to me. I had finally made friends in Upstate New York, but not all of my friends could withstand the dark shroud that was forced upon me. Some people, and you can't blame them, deal with tragedy by running away from it. Which meant they were running away from me. They didn't know what to say, what to do, how to help, or how to deal with the uncertainty. So, they just faded away.

While waiting for the surgery day to arrive, I realized there were some friends I hadn't seen in a long time. It was just too much for anyone to watch, and they knew I had my family around me. I will say that the people who stood by me during this dark period of my life are still close friends and confidantes today, and everyone of them is a very special person in my book!

At the time, however, it was hard to understand why some friends just never called or visited, but I know now that it's just the way some people deal with pain and suffering. Some people can't take it. It's understandable now, but it was confusing to me at the time.

What type of friend would I have been if I had to make a choice about seeing someone who was in my circumstances at such a young age? We were just a few years out of high school. Some of us were in college. I hope I would have tried to help them because that's what I have always done, what I learned from my amazing parents and my faith in God. That's why I'm writing this "self-help memoir" and sharing it with others out there who need to fight their way back from what they perceive as an ending. Maybe, in a way, it's a beginning?

If not for the love and friendships that were provided to me at this exact moment, I'm not sure I would be here today to tell the story. Surprisingly, the least likely people will sometimes give the most beneficial results when it comes to support, understanding, and *"stepping-up-to-the plate"* to help someone who is sick or injured. It's up to all of us to remain open-minded, hopeful, confident, and aware of the plight of others. For we never know when we will be the person who desperately needs such unconditional love.

The surgical date was rapidly approaching, and I had gotten over the boredom by trying to reconcile a million thoughts that seemed like loose ends to me. The only time my mind wasn't worrying and searching for answers was when I had a Mario Gaming Party with my loyal friends. Since I couldn't get out of bed, this worked! This is my best memory from this period of down-time, and probably why I ended up getting a degree in Game Design when I finally did go back to college. While I was controlling the character on the screen, I was somebody else … healthy, strong, and persistent.

Games have always been a part of my life … from sports and hockey to video games. Games can bring total strangers together for a common cause which helps everyone who is contributing. This was distraction for all of us. We didn't have to talk about the operation coming up or worry about each other's feelings on the subject. We could immerse ourselves in the game. It was our only focus! It's so bittersweet for me to remember now, decades later, that these friends stayed with me from start to finish. Just like in the game; no one could leave until it was completely done, totally over.

As I mentioned it was a confused, surreal time in my life. Childhood friends came all the way from New Rochelle either to check on me or say their goodbyes. Who knew? No one could anticipate what the outcome would be. There were people I expected to see who never came and then there were people I thought would never visit who showed up willing to help by any means necessary. It was perplexing but comforting at the same time. *No rhyme or reason ... but so was my health!*

March 15, 2004, that date will forever be etched in my memory.

This is the day that my life changed forever ... robotic surgery.

I couldn't believe that it had only been 3-1/2 months since New Year's Day 2004 when I thought my life was going to change for the better ... No Such Luck!

SECTION VIII

Surgery, Recuperation, Dangling by a Thread

"Why does my family have to suffer through this too?"

Chapter Thirty-one: D Day for Anthony J. Williams, III,

"Why us?"

Even though I was the one who was going through all of this, my family would be wide awake while I was sleeping through the magic of anesthesia while they worried and suffered. If something happened to me, I might never know it, but they would. I have no idea what happens when we die. No one really does, even if they've had a "near-death experience". It's still uncertain. *Maybe there is no "other side?"*

I have strong faith, as does my whole family, and I like to believe there's something else out there, that we do "go on" in some fashion, but I can't help anybody else on that score because I just don't know. I really don't think anyone really knows, no matter how many dreams and *"Eureka moments"* they think they've had to the contrary. That's just the way it is; the way it's supposed to be, I guess.

Let me start with some positives about March 15, 2004. I woke up that morning released from all the machines and Picc lines and antibiotics flooding through my system which really made me sick in a lot of ways. So, I actually felt kind of *"good"*, all things considered. I had watched the videos so many times and read everything I could find on robotic surgery and mechanical heart valves, but somehow, I still couldn't grasp how much things were going to change. It felt like a day of freedom for a moment; then, my mind flooded with all the unanswered questions to which I knew there really were no answers.

People ask me when I tell them about that morning, how I could have felt "free?" I was able to get up by myself, go to the bathroom by myself, get dressed without help, and even walk up the stairs to face my family. That was the hardest part. But, it was also the day we were going to fix this problem, one way or another.

I knew there was a chance that my dwindling body could reject the mechanical valve, and the possibility of a worst-case scenario where I would never survive the surgery. My body was weak; my heart was insufficient to sustain me; and I wasn't going to get any better than I was right now. This is where my head was at that morning.

"This was my D Day."

***

I wanted to lash out and yell and scream about the unfairness of it all, especially for my family. *"Why me? Why them? Why us? Why do my parents and sisters have to go through this? Why now? What now? What if I don't make it? What if…?"*

Yet, I plastered a big smile on my face, very slowly and gingerly walking up the stairs to greet everyone. I knew I had to make everybody laugh one more time. "Who's ready?" I snickered at them with a jokester's laugh.

I couldn't help but notice that Mom was fighting back tears. She grabbed me and hugged me like it would be the last time she held her baby boy. I almost lost it then, but I held it together somehow. Next, Dad hugged me and said, "You'll be fine; you *are* a Williams." Then, as he continued to look me dead-in-the-eye, Dad said, "Anthony, I love you; you fight! You hear me? Fight! Because we don't know how to give up."

My father was right, and I knew it. All the years came back in a flash of us banging our heads together for one silly reason or another. Dad knew how stubborn I was; the whole family knew how stubborn I was. I also knew it was time to listen to my family; so, I did.

Chapter Thirty-two, Day of Surgery, *"Positive pre-op thoughts."*

"To say that this day was a day of 'firsts' for me probably seems repetitive with all the 'firsts' I've had in my short life, but this was the 'first time' my life totally changed.

I hate to tell you at this juncture that there will be more abrupt changes, but there will be."

—Anthony J. Williams, III

***

It was a day of whirlwind activity, unanswered questions in my mind, and terrifying moments hidden behind jokes and laughter. Before I was going anywhere, I was spending some loving, cherished moments with my Rottweiler puppy, Bella. Even though she really was only a puppy, she somehow knew I needed her. So, instead of tearing around the house and chewing everything up in her path as we expect all puppies to do, Bella was glued to me, lying on my bed with me throughout my whole illness. She never left my side unless she had to go out or be walked, which Tara and Michelle promised me they would continue to do while I was gone.

After the car was packed, which brought back memories of going on family outings as a kid only my sisters weren't with us, but it looked like my parents wouldn't be going back home for quite some time. The echo of the truck door slamming shut behind me filled me with dread and emotional turmoil. So, I did what I always did when I wanted to make my parents cry with laughter, not with worry. It was time for all of us to fight, but in order to do so we had to pretend everything was going to be okay. I performed my best Jim Carey, Adam Sandler, Seinfeld, and anyone else I could mimic, which I was really good at; it made the trip go much faster, And even though the tears of laughter were also tears of fear, we didn't mention that to each other.

Columbia Presbyterian Hospital speaks for itself in New York City with a distinguished reputation. The only other time I had been here was when we met with Dr. Argenzianno to set the surgery date. I knew the drill for surgery ... I wore a special jumpsuit they had provided me with and nothing to eat or drink after 7 p.m. the night before. So, I was able to be home with my family which I greatly appreciated, and I know they did too. It really helped me emotionally and mentally I had been in hospitals and doctor's offices for so much of my life, and no one knew how long I would be in this hospital after the surgery. Like the endocarditis, it was a day-to-day process.

When I entered the hospital, I was filled with fear, but still smiling as if nothing was wrong. In the waiting area, I became quite overwhelmed and nervous. It seemed like every nurse in the hospital had to poke me again and again for bloodwork and attach wires and machines to my body. I tried really hard to just breath in and out and not get claustrophobic. I tried not to think about the fact that I was only 21 years old, and the youngest recipient of robotic surgery that Dr. Argenzianno had ever done. I clung to the fact that this doctor was the best! I tried to hang on with every positive fact I knew about this surgery, Columbia Presbyterian Hospital, and how it could save me.

In those few moments of peace and quiet, I prayed but also accepted this might be the last time I breathed, spoke, listened, and laughed with family and friends. The thought of prior obstacles and dreams were finally released. This was the only thing that meant anything at all. It always had been; I just hadn't known it before.

***

I was relieved when they let my parents come back to sit with me, but the reunion was short-lived. I was quiet, especially for me; just didn't have it in me to crack jokes. Thick emotion was hanging from every mechanical device in the room, most of them attached to me. Also, I didn't feel quite right. It wasn't something that could put into words, just a heaviness that seemed to bear down on me with dark morbidity.

I could see that my parents were feeling it too, but they smiled and gave me a pep-talk, trying to keep a conversation going that was just too difficult for me to follow. I remember smiling a lot, a goofy grin I'm sure, and nodding my head. It was about all I could manage. I was tired, exhausted in fact; I was lost in total, apprehensive fear.

I remember trying to catch my breath and couldn't. That didn't really make sense to me; they had already hooked me up to oxygen in the prep room. It would be turned off for just a few minutes when they wheeled the gurney down to the operating room. I nodded to the nurse who told me this. My parents knew the drill as well.

Finally, trying to breath, hoping I was calm and still smiling—I really didn't know whether I was or not—I shut my eyes, but kept trying to open them as the gurney was pushed and pulled out of the prep room, through corridors, and down a narrow hallway that seemed like it was closing in on me. Everything looked so dark. Why was the light fading in and out? Like there was an electrical power shortage or something.

When I could see, I saw my mother. I remember the whisper of her kisses on my face, a hint of a grin. She knew I was going to fight with everything in me!

Dad was talking to me, but I couldn't really hear him. His facial expression, however, was strong and encouraging.

They'd given me a last injection straight into the I.V. right before we left the curtained area. Maybe that was what was causing me to feel so weary and the reason for the loss of all my sensory perceptions. I felt a red-hot flush spread across my face, neck, and chest.

Then I felt a rush of adrenaline, like a burst of memories reaching all the way back to my childhood. It was like a picture book or photo album showing me all the things I'd been through, even when I was a baby, which I shouldn't have been able to remember. This happened in mere milli-seconds. My life was rushing in front of my sightless eyes.

I heard my mother gasp. Was that the last thing I remembered? No, no, the sounds! All the machines connected to my heart were clanging with alarms and sharp, harsh warnings. I was crashing! I knew this from watching the videos. My parents hadn't wanted me to see that one, but of course, I watched it the most. I had to know what was going on. It had happened, everything we all had feared … what was left of my heart valve had disintegrated; it was gone!

The last thing that I'm sure that I saw was the look on my mom's face; she was choking, sobbing. I couldn't see Dad, but I could hear his gruff, strangled, loud cries. Mom, though, she had always been my savior, my angel. My angel was devastated; her hand was over her mouth; she stumbled and leaned helplessly against the wall as everything went black.

I completely lost consciousness. No sound; no images; no smell; no taste; no pain; no feeling whatsoever. My last conscious thought:

"WAS I DEAD?"

Chapter Thirty-three: After Surgery, *"How do I accept all this?"*

"Was I supposed to die?"

—Anthony J. Williams, III

Such a philosophical question, which of course can never be hinted at or surmised. Was it all orchestrated long before I was born that I would be saved at that last final moment? So many tiny, minute things could have happened to make that wild gurney ride through the hospital corridors be one minute earlier—so that my own flesh-and-blood existing heart valve wouldn't explode—or one minute later, when it might have been too late. I keep going back to the fast-forward video of my whole life *"flashing in front of my mind's eye"*.

My operation was not the routine heart "zipper" that most people are familiar with, cut from sternum to gut and opened up like a fish. What Dr. Argenzianno did to me would be just as painful and require just as long a recovery. They would be entering my body through the ribcage on the right side, breaking a few ribs, and pulling my chest cavity apart while metallic robotic arms with a laser repaired and inserted the mechanical valve. I find it remarkable that this technology even exists, but I'm even more blown away by the fact that I survived a procedure like this as weak as I was, *and the heart valve had totally stopped working, stopped pumping blood!*

I do remember, however, at the end of surgery seeing, hearing, and sensing some things that now seem impossible. *"Were they dreams? Was I somehow mixing up past memories from previous surgeries with the current robotic operation? Or, the scariest question of them all: Was I cognizant of what was happening on a whole different level, like the stories you hear of someone's consciousness hovering in the air above their own body and being able to sense everything that was going on?"*

I was positive that I could hear voices. They were muffled and faint as if they were coming from a long distance away. I remember my eyelids feeling very heavy, but if I was thoroughly anesthetized, I shouldn't have heard anything, *right?*

I couldn't feel my limbs, but my brain seemed to be working overtime. That's the only way I can explain it. It felt like a dream within a dream or what some psychologists call *"lucid dreaming"*. My natural instinct was to open my eyes, and it seemed like my eyelids were getting lighter and lighter, but that wasn't the case. It was like big anvils of weight were hanging from my eyelashes. Somehow, even though my eyes were pasted shut, I could see a male nurse standing above the incision area, which had already been sutured and stapled shut. I also couldn't speak, but I felt like I grunted in response. The nurse was washing the area where they had ripped me totally apart.

As post-op cleanup continued, I grunted a few times. Every action that was taking place had a deep, heavy pressure to it. Not quite what I would call pain, but disturbing and seriously uncomfortable all at the same time. It seemed like an eternity of torture but was probably only a couple of seconds.

Maybe I did surface for a few moments before everything faded to black? I can't really come to grips with what was going on in that brief timespan, not then and not now. I don't know where I was, except it was in an operating theatre, the kind where other doctors, interns, nurses, and specialists could watch from a glassed alcove above. And I've never figured out how I was experiencing these things but experience them I did. *"Were they real memories or just figments of my imagination? I guess I'll never know for sure."*

It's possible that I was given more anesthesia right after the operation because I don't remember anything else until waking up in the surgical recovery area

***

I woke up—*this time for real!*—in a chair with a female nurse removing my catheter. Let me tell you, returning to full consciousness with someone's hands in your pants removing a tube from your penis is a shock no matter what the circumstances are. But, in true Anthony the class-clown charm and style, these words popped out of my mouth, "Thank God for a hot nurse!" And, it was no exaggeration, she was absolutely beautiful.

The nurse started laughing so much, she had to stop what she was doing. The next words that surfaced were, "I'm thirsty."

She handed me a juice box, but when I tried to take a sip, I couldn't shallow or even hold the juice in my mouth. We both giggled as the juice leaked out of my mouth and down my face. It was the perfect time to laugh at something funny. I was just accepting on a conscious level that I wasn't dead, and I had made it though the operation. It was great moment! One I will hold onto for the rest of my life.

The nurse finished removing the catheter and let me sit for a few brief moments, but in the upright position I was having trouble breathing. Right after I was laid back down to take the pressure off my lungs and abdomen, Dr. Oz, the well-known TV doctor and Cardiothoracic Surgeon, was standing right in front of me. Even in my weakened, foggy state I could tell he was amazed at what had just been done to me. He didn't say anything, but the look on his face said it all. I had lived to tell the story of the youngest robotic recipient of a mechanical heart valve.

My next visitor was the doctor who saved my life, Dr. Argenzianno. He had some discouraging news for me. I couldn't breathe because one of my lungs had collapsed during surgery. He prescribed meds for pain, which was coming mostly from the damaged lung at this point. The attractive nurse would stay with me and rub my chest in the collapsed lung area to help me spit up everything that was left over from the surgery. I only saw my parents briefly. They still looked frightened but they put up a brave front for me. They were gone in less than a minute.

My celebratory mood was rapidly changing to uncertain anxiety as I noticed the open wound from which a tube protruded, draining blood and excess fluid out of my chest and lungs so I could heal. I realized just before the pain meds slipped me into a coma-like sleep that even though I had survived, there was a rough road ahead for me. It would be a long time before my life would be anything close to normal, if that option even existed for me anymore. We all knew that my body could reject the mechanical valve. I drifted into unconsciousness thinking:

"Were there any other options if my body rejected the artificial valve?

I felt like my life was dangling by a mere thread!"

Chapter Thirty-Four: Reality of the Heart Valve, *"Will I reject it?"*

"It's hard to give up simple things, but simple to give up when things get hard."

Anthony J. Williams, III: *"This has become my life's motto!"*

Wow! Back in January when I was restricted to a room in a small hospital in Dutchess County, Up State New York, hooked to a big machine being everyone's pin cushion for blood tests twice every hour and terrified by something called "endocarditis", I created my life's motto to remind me of how strong I needed to be to beat the bacterial heart infection.

Now here I am on March 15, 2004, and I find myself thinking about my life's motto, but this time with fear and helplessness. It would be so easy just to give up, but I'll never, ever do that to my family. They're counting on me to fight, fight, fight and win just one more time! *"Can I do it? Am I strong enough with all that I've been through? I really didn't know..."*

This very first robotic surgery to put a mechanical heart valve in someone as young as I was had no track record, no guarantee, no studies to show us the road ahead. It was all unknown territory ... for me, my family, even Dr. Argenzianno. My body could reject this mechanical valve at any moment with no warning. Would it *crash* like my real heart valve did when we were rushing through the halls of

Columbia Presbyterian Hospital in New York City to get me on the operating table? What if it happened in the middle of the night and no one was around? Because I didn't remember anything after my *real* heart valve stopped working, just the sound of all those alarms going off and then I felt nothing at all. *"Is that what it's going to be like?"*

I knew I needed to re-evaluate the consequences of giving up, giving in, letting go, not fighting back. The real "fight" was just beginning. The surgery had merely been Act I. The rest of the story still had to be written, and there was no battle plan or outline to follow.

I thought about the first part of my motto: I really did miss the simple things of life, like buttoning up my own shirt or rolling over in bed, holding a paper cup or a fork or spoon without shaking like an old guy with palsy, washing my face and shaving, but most of all "standing on my own two feet!" That was going to take a while. Everything was going to *"take a long while to learn again, feel comfortable with again, to become automatic the way everyone else does **normal everyday** activities. I just can't "give up when things get hard." Everyone is counting on me to be the Super Mario Hero!*

"Dear Lord," I prayed all that day and long into the night, **"Give me strength!"**

***

I was supposed to rest and sleep as much as I could right after the operation. *Yeh, right, a little tough to do with round-the-clock monitoring and blood tests being done every half-hour to check for all kinds of things: infection, internal bleeding, changes in my blood chemistry that could indicate all sorts of problems.* I got to see my parents, but only briefly for a few precious seconds, but I was still very much *"out-of-it"* anyway.

The first 12 hours after surgery were crucial from the standpoint of recovery from such an invasive procedure, but more importantly to look for any sign that my body was rejecting the foreign object that had been placed in my living, beating heart.

I'm not exactly sure when I became obsessed with listening to every beat of my heart. Maybe as soon as I came of surgery; maybe even before—the memories that kept surfacing where I was able to see and hear the doctors and nurses in the O.R. while still under anesthesia; my eyelids too heavy to open. This has bothered me for a long time. I try not to think about it.

Probably, however, it was when my elation at having survived the procedure was replaced with dread for an uncertain future. It was like I was hearing the ticking of a clock counting down the seconds of my life with the beat of my damaged heart. When it got to be too much for me, I had the power of the morphine drip to ease the pain, help with the tube in my chest which was causing me to itch like crazy from the stitches, and go to sleep to hide from it all. Yet, I would be jolted awake from a deep sleep hearing and feeling my heartbeat. It was going to take some time getting used to hearing it, predicting it, living with it. Time was on my side. Every heartbeat that coincided with a breath was encouragement to keep fighting and keep going!

Luckily being young and in relatively good health, all things considered, prior to the endocarditis and subsequent heart valve damage, was positive in many ways. If nothing else, it gave me an ideal for which to strive. Maybe because of my youth and prior strength, the collapsed lung seemed to heal rather quickly after Dr. Argenzianno switched to another medicine that worked really well, and don't forget I had the cutest nurse in New York City tapping and massaging my chest to remove fluid/tar buildup from the long surgery. It was the first little victory that gave me a taste of achievement. If I had known then, though, what I would learn after—how hard this recuperation was going to be—I probably wouldn't have felt it was a victory at all.

I tried to keep up a good front for my folks, laughing at myself and calling myself Frankenstein from the scars and tracks and tape bandages and open chest wound. One memory that surfaced, however, I didn't share with anyone and I didn't laugh about was when I heard my heart beating all the time. It reminded me of the end of the movie "Hook" after he's been beaten by Peter Pan, the look on the illain's face with the endless ticking clocks that at first people could "hear" in a ilent room. This scene wouldn't let go of me, and it really messed with my head. I eeded to find new jokes and funny material to get through that image which aunted me. When the beating of my heart got too much for me, I thought about ow good it was just to be alive.

The first couple of days I was by myself and I slept a lot, but after that I had a roommate. The only way to keep myself laughing was to try and get my revolving roommates to laugh too, but in a hospital like Columbia Presbyterian the cases are very traumatic. It opened my eyes to the suffering of others, going through multiple surgeries, pain, and the same struggle I was enduring. I know that much of my empathy for fellow human beings and wanting to reach out and help others as much as I can, even in the writing of my own life story, comes from these experiences.

I remember all too well my first tentative steps as I began to try and walk the hallways. Each step I took forward wasn't a step back backward. Being the youngest recipient of a mechanical heart valve through robotic placement meant I was also the youngest person in the unit. Everyone else was like in their 60s or more, but I was *just* as decrepit at first as we all were.

The good news is that as the days continued to add up, my body was ***not*** rejecting the heart valve. That was the most important news I could be given every day, and I always asked. My parents were told more than I was, of course, but the always leveled with me.

After walking the hallways, I started physical therapy. The stairs were really a challenge, but I took everything in stride and found a way to make a joke about it. Fun was very limited in this environment, so I took advantage of every silly thing that popped into my head to entertain myself, the nurses, even my roommates whether they laughed or not, and the Physical Therapists.

I might have been suffering and crying on the inside, but I'd let very few people see how much it was getting to me as I listened to my heartbeat day and night or had recurring nightmares about the odd sequence of events in the operating room at the end of the procedure. Somehow, I made peace with both of these disturbing incidents, but I have to admit it was long after the hospital and recuperation at home before I adjusted to these odd experiences which I will never forget.

I felt I was ready to leave the hospital much sooner than the medical professionals would allow. All of my vital organs had to function properly, which meant going to the bathroom by myself and completing all the torture-chamber challenges of physical therapy. I always was motivated by laughter, so I carried on making fun of every little thing that came my way. Also, I never let go of the fact that I had survived and my body had not rejected the valve, but I couldn't wait to get home to my own bed, to cuddle with Bella my dear puppy, and be with my loving family and friends once again. *Sounds idyllic, right? NOT SO!*

I didn't realize how tough it was going to be at home. I should have remembered how difficult it had been at first going home with endocarditis and being totally bedridden, having my mom take me to the bathroom, dress me like a baby, feed me in bed, and give me a bath hooked up to a huge machine that kept me prisoner. I had become downright belligerent! And the infection had just been the warmup routine. I had no idea how much harder this homecoming was going to be, but all that mattered right now was that I'd made it. I had to hold on to that precious, God-given miracle.

Chapter Thirty-five: Going Home, *"Was I hoping for normal again?"*

I don't know how I expected everything to be normal, like waving a magic wand, as soon as I came home from the hospital. If anything, it was even more upsetting than the hospital because I knew Columbia Presbyterian was a temporary situation. Going home in my mind meant *"going back to the way things were before."* It was a rude awakening for me mentally and emotionally to realize I was a 21-year old guy with an uncertain future. This affected me so much more than the physical aspects of healing. I was still keeping up my front of being the comedian and hiding the insecurities that were plaguing me my every waking moment. This was all uncharted territory.

I was given a teddy bear to hug, holding him tight against my chest, every time I had to cough. I needed to take blood thinners which left me very much aware of being careful not to fall with my weak, awkward gait, not to tumble out of bed, not to roughhouse with the guys who came to see me. All of the sudden, I was delicate and weak, and I could see it in the eyes and on the faces of my friends and family. I was different, and I was going to remain *different*. Even my diet had to be closely monitored, something I had never given a thought to before.

Yet, still, the biggest fear that constantly gnawed at me day and night was the constant sound and feel of my heart beating. It kept me from sleeping at night. It woke me up in the morning. It never allowed me to rest completely.

All of these changes took time and perseverance on my part, but I was motivated to walk again without assistance, to conquer the constant pain, to deal with all the drugs I had to take, and not cringe when I saw the fear in my mother's eyes which she tried to hide behind a smile. Just as before, she was caring for me herself, and I wasn't always the most cooperative patient. I was starting my life all over again from scratch, and there was no rule book to guide me on my way.

I had to continue to hold onto the positive facts. I had survived. I had beat the odds. The future might be different, but at least there was a future. I was very lost and confused, but I was still fighting back. My family was so supportive. I had to get my head together for them.

***

I didn't realize at first that I wasn't the only one who could hear my heart beating. It wasn't just in my head. It was right there in the room beside me. With a mechanical valve if someone is sitting next to me and it's relatively quiet, they too can hear my heart beating.

I remember one of the first nights after I got home while I was sitting at the kitchen table. My niece kept looking at me with a confused look on her face. I asked her what was wrong. She asked, "I hear something; does anyone else hear that? It sounds like *clicking*."

I pasted a fake smile on my face and answered her as best I could, "It's my heart; it sounds like a clock." She gently pressed her ear and sweet, concerned face over my heart and her eyes grew enormous. She glued her head to my chest for minutes, it seemed, to listen. She was mesmerized by the addictive, calming tone.

As time heals all wounds, so does time soothe the unexpected and ease the all too obvious. I don't even hear the clicking sound anymore. Sometimes I notice when other people hear it, but I'm no longer afraid or upset by it. The clicking of my heart is life itself … my life.

This was a huge transition for me. I had to give up all my dreams of playing hockey, even as a recreational sport as I would all sports, and I had to learn to live with all the changes this mechanical heart valve had brought me. It was a long process, and one that I suffered and endured in silence. My family had been through enough already. This was my cross to bear, and somehow, someway, I found the courage and fortitude to embrace the altered person I had become.

This was the process that the video tapes of the operation never showed. The physical healing had a certain timeline to follow. The emotional and mental lerance was so much harder to learn to live with. My moods were up and down,

ut carefully hidden as well. I wouldn't let anyone into my private world where I

aced this all by myself. I prayed; I thought about it constantly; I denied it; I fought

t; and finally, I accepted it. *"What other choice did I have?"*

"It seemed that every few years there would a forced unequivocal

change in my life.

I knew I would have to reinvent myself every time or lose myself

completely."

SECTION IX

<u>The Dawning of a New Day, a New Life</u>

"I made a lot of mistakes. Why? Because I'm

me!"

Chapter Thirty-six: My Future was Mine to Create, *"A Huge Error!"*

This is going to be one of the hardest sections in this book for me to share because I'm not very proud of the person I allowed myself to become. Hard for me to admit, but there it is in black- and-white, so it must be true, *right?* Afterall, this is my own personal story. *"No one knows better than me all the wrong things to do because I did them all!"*

I have no one to blame but myself, but I know this is one of the most important, yet difficult, parts of my life to talk about. I'm doing this to help others think things through a little better than I did, and hopefully, you can find the courage to make more informed decisions, allowing others to guide you on this journey called "life". The paths are narrow and filled with pitfalls. Sometimes you just can't navigate them all alone, no matter hard you try.

***

"Indecision was foreign territory for me, but it did teach me for the first time in my life

how to get comfortable with being uncomfortable."

—Anthony J. Williams, III

I had been through it all—a heart murmur that dictated what I could and couldn't do as a kid; a blood disease that took me out of the game for a while; injuries; losing my one and only dream of playing professional hockey by totally messing up at a major university as well as a community college; endocarditis, a bacterial infection; heart surgery with the robotic implant of mechanical valve with all the changes it made in my future prospects.

I really didn't know which way to turn, but I thought I had to figure everything out for myself. I was just too blind to see the loving family and incredible support system that was standing right in front of me. I was also just too damn stubborn to listen to anyone because I thought I already knew everything there was to know about the road ahead. *"Just look what I had been through; look what I had survived? I was invincible. I was a Super Hero!"*

Right before New Year's Day 2004 when my health collapsed completely and death stared me in the eye at every turn, I had decided to go into Real Estate. I liked the flexibility of setting my own schedule so I could have plenty of goof-off time with my friends when I wanted it, the idea of very large commission checks with minimum work involved, and I had actually put in the time and effort to get my Real Estate license, so I had accomplished something. At least that was my reasoning at the time. *"Boy, was I ever off-base this time, and not just in the job market."*

In my insecurity and fear, yeah, I made a lot of mistakes. I was trying to find love in all the wrong places; trying to find the "right" woman to spend one's life with is not done with a cast of female FWBs *(friends with benefits)*. Here I had the most incredible example to follow by just opening my eyes and looking at my parents. I didn't even think what they had been through with me after the surgery and recuperation was all over. I just got lost in myself. I didn't see their devotion and love for each other and for all three of their children: Michelle, Tara, and me.

The family had really been through the wringer. Tara and her husband were going through a divorce, and Michelle and Gabby, who was injured so severely he could never walk again in a freak car accident; well, their marriage couldn't weather all that trauma either. And everyone's concern for me. *"I don't even need to go there!"*

I wasn't mentally and emotionally prepared for any type of relationship. But how do you tell someone that maybe you *could care about* that I had a time bomb anyone could hear ticking in my chest, my heart, as soon as they got within a few feet of me? To me, it just wasn't fair!

I was sure the deck had been stacked against me; that perhaps God had forsaken me? I couldn't and wouldn't accept that most of my failures were my own arrogant, egotistical fault. It took me quite a while to figure it all out and as usual I had to learn everything the hard way; unfortunately, the ***real hard way.*** I want to apologize to all my readers for what I have to put them through in what is to come

Yet, I pray, literally, that if I can help even one person out there look in the mirror and see a version of themselves at this point in my life staring back at them, I sincerely hope they can grow up a little bit, swallow their pride, and seek help before their lives completely fall apart. Because that's exactly what *"I did to myself!"*

Let me put here also in permanent *black-and-white*, an apology to all of my family members and many of my friends. Without you guys beside me, willing to love me in spite of all of my shenanigans and self-deprecating schemes and failures and addictions, I wouldn't be here right now struggling to tell my story to help the other stubborn loners out there who think they have to do everything on their own. I had been hiding so much for so long, since I was just a little boy, that it was what came natural to me. Paint on a clown's glowing smile and keep telling jokes. That way no one ever really knows what you're really up to.

This seems like the right place to admit, first off, that it wasn't until after I started writing this manuscript at 37 years old that I finally had the courage to tell my parents about the abuse I had suffered from a family member as a young child. They were shocked, but they were there for me, and they would have been there for me when it happened. It wasn't my fault, and they would have loved me just as much, just as unconditionally, just as they always have. *"But I didn't know."*

"Yeah, I was really good at hiding my fears and sorrows behind the face of a fool…"

Chapter Thirty-seven: Pathway to Destruction, *"How did I get lost?"*

"Humility: A tool that was left out of the box, not on purpose,
but due to my own lack of knowledge."

—Anthony J. Williams, II

For the first couple of years after the surgery, it may have appeared to everyone, on the surface of course, that I had found my way and my future in the Real Estate business. I seemed to be very appreciative of life, family, friends, and my career choice. I demonstrated a mature sense of control and the motivation to live life to the fullest with each successive day better than the previous day. But, the part of me that I had never allowed anyone to see or know about where all my hurts and failures were hidden did not cease; actually, I became even more proficient at disguising the ugly truths that dwelled within me.

As my Real Estate career began to blossom, perhaps partly because I knew how to *"turn on the charm"* which had always just come natural to me, but also it had been honed to perfection from my time spent with Aunt Sue, my Godmother, as a child model. I was charismatic and on-fire with new opportunities, new friends, and a new game plan!

Unfortunately, not all of the new things I initiated were in my best interest. *In fact, almost everything was "not in my best interest."*

Selling Real Estate brought in fat checks, but it also fueled a party lifestyle. Money gave those of us in the business a reason to celebrate, which included alcohol in excess and plentiful recreational drugs. I indulged in everything that came my way, like a garbage disposal—*"just load me up with anything that's available."* I would try anything once; well, truthfully, more than once because rarely did I turn anything down that I could drink, snort, or flush in pill form down my throat. I never backed away from a way to get high to drown out the emotional conflict that was stewing inside of me.

In my early 20s, I thought I was immortal, especially after the drugs kicked in. My whole existence, ever since I'd been a kid, was just wrong and unfair. The rage and anger were continuing to grow, getting darker by the day. *I was like a Malatov cocktail getting ready to explode! The "garbage disposal" was tossed in the air, spilling its tainted contents into every aspect of my life.*

This was a party scene like I had never seen before, not at this magnitude. I had dappled a little in pot and of course, drinking, but the euphoria of this fast-paced crowd was like hitting the jackpot or winning a hockey game/season/final. I knew all about ego and competition. I had always thrived on it! At least, I thought I did, but this was a whole new level of debauchery that had really never occurred to me in my wildest dreams. I thought it was safe and accepted. Afterall, I was the young guy, and these were adults acting this way, *which make it okay, right?*

The next five years of my life would be the darkest days I had ever known, and what was really sad about the whole experience was that I was the last to realize there was anything wrong with me. No matter how hard I tried, it was engrained in me that I had reached for the stars and come up empty handed so many times. I really hadn't worked through the deep-seeded sense of losing everything I had ever wanted—my dream of playing professional hockey, wasting my education at Iona Prep School on not one, but two colleges; my health and wellbeing; and my self-esteem. I didn't value myself as a person anymore, so I had to find ways to dull the throbbing pain.

The only competition I was embroiled in was within myself. I was so used to not getting what I wanted that it was just easier for me to accept "not winning". I thought it was a harsh, but true fact of life. *"No one ever gets what they want, so why try so hard when the outcome is always going to be the same?"*

I concluded that this happened to everyone, but especially *"Anthony J. Williams, III."* So why fight it? I intended to have as much fun as I could for as long as possible because the future had nothing to offer *"Me!"* I was superficial, arrogant, egotistical, and hopelessly lost.

I'm not even sure when the realization of this faulty reasoning sunk in my addled mind to the point where I just gave up trying and reached out for everything that was opposite of how I had been raised and what I had once perceived my own values to be. I can't think of one defining moment when it all came together. It was just there; it had taken ahold of me and wouldn't let me go. Each step I took was further and further away from everything I had ever aspired to be.

Looking back now, I'm not sure I even knew who that guy was ... the one *with a chip on his shoulder* that was supposed to be me. There was no rhyme or reason to the actions I put into play or the habits I acquired that became serious, life-threatening addictions. I had been through so much, but I literally threw it all away.

It all seemed the same to me—winning and losing. I couldn't tell one from the other. If I had money to spend on booze, sex, drugs, then that was good; if I didn't have money, I suffered from my addictions, but there were always friends to help me out, *which was good, right?* I kept getting in deeper and deeper. The highs were high, but the lows were unbearable.

My inability to tell the difference between what was positive and what was negative in my life was abruptly thrust upon me with no warning whatsoever. The confusion left me cold, callus, and cynical.

My sarcasm and mimicking had always been the funny-guy Anthony, the silly kid who made everyone laugh. Now it became my coping mechanism to hide my personal secrets. *But hadn't I really been doing this my whole life? And I really wasn't fooling anyone.*

Chapter Thirty-eight: Influence of Friends, *"Was it my downfall?"*

I already had friends in Up-State New York, but the Real Estate profession brought new workmates that I felt I had to outshine and impress. After all, I was the new guy, and I had to prove myself in a very *dog-eat-dog business.* You had to keep up in the sales arena, but you also had to become part of the team that *partied-hearty.* At least, it looked that way to me. Besides, it was just plain fun, and after what I'd been through, I thought I was ready for something new and exciting! I didn't think we were really hurting anyone, just blowing off steam at the end of the day.

I can look back now and see that my method of being accepted wasn't quality, but rather quantity. I was like the garbage disposal of buying, selling, renting, and quick turnovers. I took anything I could get my hands on. All the stuff the established agents didn't want to touch because they knew it just wasn't worth it. As usual, I had to learn the hard way.

I would take anything at any time with no thought at all to the fact that I was still recovering from heart surgery. This relates not only to working, but to alcohol and drugs as well. I just wanted to numb the pain and fear, stay busy, be considered part of the group, and fill the void that my life had become after failing at so many other endeavors—higher education, the decline of my health which had kept me isolated for so long, and the loss of my life-long dream.

In some ways, I guess, I was just bored, scared, angry. I felt cheated! Addiction was already knocking at my door; in fact, I had already let it in and was entrenched, even though I thought I could handle it and stop it whenever I wanted. Yet, I couldn't see any reason to stop. I was grown up now; I was an adult. This was the dramatic, ritzy lifestyle that I had been denied by being so sick for such a long time.

I torched some good friendships and relationships because I thought I was in a league above them because I had money. And money brought drugs, alcohol, get-togethers with high rollers, and a whole new bag of tricks just ripe for the taking by a greedy, selfish, and disillusioned kid just trying to catch up with everything. I felt I had lost my individuality during the shut-in incarceration in my room because of endocarditis and the long time it took to recuperate from having my whole body torn apart to put a foreign object, the mechanical valve, in my heart. I don't know why I never thought about how much love and support my family had given me, especially my mom who devotedly cared for me. It just never crossed my mind because my thoughts were on a different wavelength. I had already tuned into a different master … the slave of addiction.

I was thrilled to become the protégé of Anthony Serino. He was always there for me as someone to look up to in business, someone to learn from, and I wanted to be just like him. He was married, and his wife was happy to let me hangout with them or tagalong when they went to parties to applaud the closing on a big property deal or even a small success. It didn't matter. Every sale was a time for rejoicing. The nature of the business was that we always had something to celebrate. Anthony and his wife were totally respected in the Real Estate community. I thought they had it all, and they did, but they and other friends I made during this crazy, unleashed phase of my life would introduce to me to a lifestyle filled with alcohol and illegal drugs. Anthony, however, would be my mentor through the tough times and later on through good times as well.

I became *"best friends"* with Jason "Jay" Coyne and his twin brother Matt. They were really close in age to me. As a garbage disposal in the recreational substance area as well as the job, I liked to snort, smoke, and drink: fancy, expensive liquor and wines; cocaine, crack, pills, and marijuana. With all I'd been through medically, needles had little or no appeal to me, but not so with Jay. He really enjoyed PCP, as well as other substances you had to *"shoot up"* to experience the maximum effect. He loved it and was a party onto himself when he was flying high!

My buddy Jay should have been my wakeup call, but I was already too far gone, too addicted, when Bob, Jay's older brother, called me to tell me that Jay had gotten trashed on a combination of drugs including PCP in their living room. Jay's mother found him dead sitting in the chair where he had overdosed. I remember grasping the phone and falling to my knees in tears and pain. I couldn't stand, couldn't talk, couldn't understand. I think about Jay's poor mother more now than I did back then; how could she ever forget the sight of her son, her baby, one of her twins dead from a wicked, lethal habit? There are some hurts that never go away, even in retrospect.

I was dating and engaged to a great girl, Amanda. She had quite an impact on me. This is another time when I should have seen that my addictions were coming between me and the *"happily every after"* that I wanted for my life. When she couldn't take my erratic behavior anymore, I blamed her. Just another sad and remorseful event in my life that was full of such things. I know now that Amanda taught me how to love another human as a true human being, a lesson that has stayed with me my whole life and is such a part of my marriage now as well as being a father to the best son and daughter I could ever have hoped to help bring into this world. So, I learned some lessons back then; I just couldn't see it at the time.

There is just no way to see what is happening to you when addiction takes over. There is no bias or emotion involved in addiction, just the motive to get more, do more, experience higher highs, and keep right on sinking deeper and deeper into the trap from which there is no escape. This is all I thought about, and it totally consumed me. I got to the point where I didn't even care about the surgery that had saved my life. Even though I had lost my best friend, Jay, it still didn't dawn on me that I could be next.

Everyone around me could see what was happening. My father started following me every weekend after I left the house so he could see who I was hanging with and what we were doing. He challenged me with similar words to what he told me when I went in for surgery, "We don't give up, Anthony. We fight that's what we do; that's what we've always done. I'm not going to give up on you and I don't want you to give up either!"

Little did Dad know that at the time I was seriously contemplating suicide I just couldn't see any other way out, and I truly wasn't aware of what addiction does to your mental and emotional outlook: depression, manic episodes o uncontrollable laughter which makes no sense, sadness and tears that come out o nowhere when you least expect them. It wears you down with each step you tak on the path, but you can always find something else to pin it on or someone else t blame. You never look in the mirror and see the real image that has become "you" I got sloppy with my clothes and my grooming. I didn't care how I looked. became harder and harder to keep the party going, yet I felt I had to keep up wit everyone else. This is the lifestyle I had chosen, and *"Hey, look at all the co friends it brought me!"*

I was in a downward spiral from which there is no return; not on my own was in a dark, dangerous place like a maze or a labyrinth with no end in sight a no way out. There was no key to the puzzling turns that would eventually lead me to surface because there was no path back to where I had come from. It didn't exist.

Addiction is baffling, confusing, and cunning. Talking to my dad should have been the first step to recovery, but addiction doesn't work that way. There are no saviors. There is only destruction. There is no way to romance addiction. It claims its own.

I remember it was on Thanksgiving Day with my family; we met at my sister Michelle's house. I didn't know it at the time, but that would be the last holiday I was with my family for some time. I fell asleep in the living room and don't even remember the family atmosphere that I had grown up with. The lights were getting ready to go out in my life. Once the fire burns out, the flames that fuel the "need" for more drugs, more alcohol—there is no going back. My family realized that day that they had to save the light before it burnt out forever.

***

Dad woke me up that next Saturday morning, telling me he "needed my help in the yard." When I got upstairs in the kitchen, I noticed a stranger there, a Mexican guy named Jimmy. I exploded when I saw him! I went into an uncontrollable rage. Jimmy was himself a recovering addict. He was the interventionist. My inclination was to run, get out, escape!

My car was blocked in by all the other cars in the family. Tara and Michelle were there too. Everyone knew I was an addict and had been for some time, except ne. There were letters written by my family members telling me that I would no longer be welcomed in their homes if I didn't get help. The writing was distraught, frightened, but firm. I would lose my family if I did not go with "Jimmy" to get help. This was my one and only chance to redeem myself. The letters told me how much they loved me. This wasn't something they wanted to do, but something they had to do. I knew it was all true. It descended upon me like a dark shroud blocking out the sun, but in my heart the addiction was still pulling at me, still possessing me. *How could I decide?*

Yet, I did decide, and I did get help. How many others never get that chance? How many addicts never have a family to intervene? *I didn't know it at the time, but I had been blessed.*

I wanted to stop this again when I learned it was a 90-day program in California. I argued that I had to delay. *"Not now,"* I said, *"not yet; not today; not so far away from everyone I know!"*

I had to go with Jimmy right then and there to catch a flight to California to a place called "A Better Tomorrow." It was quite a struggle and much arguing back and forth, but they were right. My whole family was right. I couldn't do this myself. How could I cure something that I didn't even know existed? I finally agreed to go. I was so afraid; I can't even begin to tell you how terrified, lost, and alone I felt.

I had the love and understanding of others that I really didn't deserve, but I thank God that I did. In many ways, this book started out as a therapeutic vehicle for me to understand myself. The more I wrote, the more I knew I had to help others. I hope these words reach the people who need them, and they will resonate with those individuals who need this love and support. I give it freely, and I'm here for you.

I was very fortunate to have the family and friends that I have. People like Steven, Kurt, Brian, Rog, Matt, Kristen, Sarah, Kerry, and even Anthony Serino. He continued to be my friend and mentor for many years to come. Unfortunately, I have to end this beautiful moment with some sad, very sad news. Just last year, Anthony Serino fell into deep depression and hopelessness. He could not see a future for himself. A little over a year after he and his wife divorced, he took his own life. I was utterly and completely devastated by his suicide. I still am. I think of him often. Sometimes even when we turn things around, the darkness can return and overwhelm us so we just can't go on anymore.

"Anthony, if I never got a chance to tell you or if you never heard me say it

before,

'I love you, man; I always will'…"

—Anthony J. Williams, III

Testimonial by Michelle, Anthony's Oldest Sister

It all began in July of 1982 when my Mom and Dad brought home this little blue-eyed baby boy. I was so excited to see him and touch him. I always wanted to help change his diaper and help my mom clean the umbilical cord. Then one day it fell off and I thought I broke him! I freaked out, but my mom assured me he would be just fine.

I took him under my wing and protected him as I felt I needed to, being his "big sister". We had a normal childhood. Mom was a stay at home mom when we were young while Dad worked hard. We lived in a nice neighborhood and were blessed with many necessities with the least amount of struggle. It was a happy, normal childhood.

Over some time, many things changed. I made Anthony an uncle when he was only 13. He loves his niece so much. He was in awe of her, and they were somewhat close in age. Anthony was still a child and in his teens as well as being in the midst of puberty. He was playing hockey all the time and getting into trouble for playing against the garage and in the basement.

When Anthony was about 14, I had gotten married and moved out on my own with my daughter. Here is where I lost some time with Anthony. I did not see him as much and lost touch with him somewhat. That is part of growing up, unfortunately; some leave and some stay, but it made it another hurdle in life because we are all super inexperienced with these hurdles in the beginning stages.

It wasn't until Anthony was about 25 that I started to notice something was wrong. He came to my house for Thanksgiving and slept more than he socialized and then left a few times, coming back in worse shape than when he'd left. I approached my parents at this time and told them that he needed help. He was looking sickly and was just not himself. We all knew he was dabbling, but we were all unaware of how much and how serious this was.

Prior to Thanksgiving I was having some weird dreams. I could not place it or why I would be having these dreams. I kept dreaming of a bat with these eyes that looked just like my brothers. The bat would fly around me, then latch onto my shirt and stare at me with these helpless eyes crying out for help. Once I seen Anthony at Thanksgiving, I knew my dream was telling me that Anthony was in trouble. My dreams have always been messages for my whole life, and I knew this was a message that could not be ignored.

Shortly after that I got a call from my mom that my brother had been arrested as he was doing 90 on the Taconic Parkway with drug paraphernalia in his vehicle. I told my mom about the dream at this point and told her that the dream was just confirming the urgency of the matter at hand and that we needed to do something before it was too late. I told her, "Mom, you will be burying your son, and I will be saying goodbye to my one and only brother, if we don't act on this."

So, my sister and I started looking places up for treatment online. Mom then looked into her insurance to see what they had as options as well. Ultimately as a family we made the decision that he needed help and that he needed to get out of the area in order for it to be successful. We made the call, and it was all set up to happen. We needed to continue our daily routines as to not let him in on anything out of the ordinary. This was breaking my mom's heart, and she was so distraught over this, but it had to be done to keep him alive.

The day of the intervention came way too fast. We all had to have a letter written to Anthony from us with how much we loved him and what we would not accept as far as his usage and the future. Basically, we had to tell him if he would not get help, he could not have any of us in his life. Being a parent myself I know this killed my parents to have to say this to him. I know this tore me to pieces which is a feeling that I will never ever forget.

Anthony reacted out of anger and frustration and stormed to his room. The interventionist followed to talk him down and get him to reason. Anthony refused and came out of his room ready to leave. I am assuming he was going to get a fix to make him forget what he was dealing with at the moment. My father refused to let the one and only chance we had to get Anthony help and started fighting with him to keep him there. This was traumatic to all of us as emotions were so high and the unknown was so very scary. Would he go to treatment or would he die in a few years? This was our only chance to keep him ALIVE!!!!!!!!

Even though the Intervention was mentally and emotionally draining in a way you will never forget, it was the best day ever as I was not going to lose my brother to drugs. We had a chance to save him and that was more than most people get.

This journey was LONG for both us and Anthony, but I have to say that I am so overwhelmed with happiness to be able to speak with Anthony on the phone, Facetime, and visit when I can. I am so happy that he chose US over DRUGS. He LOVED us more than he loved getting high.

I could not put into words how very proud I am of Anthony as there are not words to describe the dedication it took to change the habits that were killing him slowly. But I can say that I am proud of the man he has become, the man he has chosen to be, the father and husband and brother and son he is today. He is truly an inspiration, and his story alone is one of success and willpower against the demons and temptations that we all live amongst.

Chapter Thirty-nine: Detox, *"What did I expect? I had no idea!"*

I'm not sure exactly when it all came to light how the "intervention" was orchestrated. Evidently some of my friends that I'd known for a while, not the group I was partying with, went to my family and expressed their concern for me. I really didn't need to know who or why or where or how come. We would talk that all through when the time was right, when and *if* it was all over, or in some cases, in the years to come.

Tara and Michelle wasted no time, immediately searching for treatment centers and how to accomplish an intervention that might work in getting through to me. My sisters took all their findings to my parents and together they found "A Better Tomorrow". Jimmy flew out from California to meet with my family and walk them through the process, discussing options and possible outcomes. Not all of them favorable, by any means.

Thankfully, my family still believed in me even during my darkest hour. They prayed as a family for divine guidance. No intervention will work unless the addict is committed to do the hard work it takes to fight the way back from crippling addiction, and detox is hell; there's just no other way to put it.

That Saturday as I read the letters from my sisters expressing their love and prayers for me, it dawned on me that I had stopped praying; something I used to do very day of my life. It filled me with sadness and shame, but eventually it would also bring me strength.

***

The flight landed in Los Angeles, California. I had never been there before. It was in the middle of the night, but the weather was warm, not at all like the winter snows of Up-State New York. I was welcomed by palm trees and a short, portly man named Al with a cheery disposition. Jimmy had told me the drive to the facility was over an hour. A lot of time for me to think about so many things—my family, my friends, all the challenges I had already been through.

I remember wondering what this "hospital" would be like because in my experience that's the only reference I had to an institution of this sort. I was starting to feel the effects of not having had any drugs at all for almost a full day, which heightened the dread of my unknown future. I had come this far, and there was no way out, no way home, no one to help me. This was an all-or-nothing situation; it was either this or certain death, sooner rather than later. I immediately thought about my best "new" friend Jay and his mother finding him stone silent in their living room. She must have thought he was sleeping until she tried to wake him. I wondered if his body was cold when she touched him? Yet my mind's eye couldn't see the horror of my family finding me that way. Not yet, not with my brain and my body still clogged with all the "garbage" I had put in it.

Jimmy and Al rode in the front seat of the vehicle; me in the backseat. They'd taken my phone away from me, my contact to outside world and everything I knew. Here I was three thousand miles away from everything and everyone I had ever known. I started to panic!

Trying to hold onto something real and solid in my life, I asked Jimmy if I could use his phone to make one last phone call to my ex-fiancèe Amanda. He wasn't supposed to let me do this, but Jimmy had been in my place and understood my need to hear her voice. Also, captive in the car like I was, there was no way I could use her as an accomplice to help me escape.

I was so relieved when she answered the phone, not knowing this out-of-state number. My family or one of our friends must have contacted her too, probably when this intervention was being organized. We had been broken up for a while now, but I knew she cared about me. And I cared about her. I explained as quickly as I could what was going on. She cried and sobbed for 10 minutes on the phone. It brought back all my tender feelings for her, but I didn't know how we could ever weather this storm, especially since we had broken our engagement because I couldn't live up to the responsibilities of being a man ready for marriage. After 10 minutes, Jimmy told me my time was done, and I had to hang up. I was sobbing too by this time.

The reality of what I had done to myself and all the people around me, especially my family and Amanda, flooded my emotions like kicking me in the teeth. *"How could I have done such a thing to everyone I loved? How could I ever break through the thick fog that clouded my mind and my heart? How could I ever be normal again? Isn't that what I'd always fought for, and I threw it all away! I was going to be alone for the first time in my life—no family, no fiancée, no friends, no one to help me. I would have to do this all by myself.*

For the first time in quite some time, I reached out for help through prayer,

"Please, God, let me survive; that's all I ask…"

***

Somewhere along the way, we stopped to grab something to eat at a fast-food chain I didn't recognize, In-N-Out Burger. This is evidently "the place to go" in California. For me, it was like being in a foreign country. I didn't realize it then, but it would surface during my treatment that I thought New York was the only place in the world and everywhere else was second-best or less. I had never thought of myself as snobbish or closed-minded. I had an awful lot to learn and unlearn.

When we pulled up to the "detox house", I started to panic again. I was going to be "processed" into the program. Images of someone being roughly handled, strip-searched, and booked for breaking the law crushed down on me. My thoughts were scattered all over the place, and none of them seemed to make any sense. I was silent and lost as they took me inside.

Everyone seemed friendly and accommodating during the introduction. It was quiet, too quiet, but everyone was sleeping under a strict curfew. We had to get used to a schedule. I was going to have to share a room with someone. My mind again went to the worst-case scenario that I would be locked up with a crazed, cruel maniac.

The first person I met in detox was Ricky, a young kid hooked on heroin. I woke him up when I put my bags down near the bed. We started talking, and he was just a regular guy, like me. We had an instant connection that helped me so much then and even now. Ricky and I became best friends, and we still are today. He is my son's godfather. I can't begin to tell you how Ricky eased my insane, frightened nerves during the tense situations that were to follow. He claims that I helped him just as much. We were trying to save our own lives. We were starting all over again.

I knew I was in a dangerous place, and everything would be a test. But initially my mind was so fuzzy, I was numb. The feelings of remorse and guilt would take a while to surface, but I still felt them in that compartment of my brain where I have always hidden the secrets that haunt me in the dark of night like sharp knives stabbing me in the heart. It took awhile to even admit what substances I had been abusing. My parents had told Jimmy what they knew—marijuana, alcohol, and perhaps cocaine. My parents had no idea the extent of my addiction. There was so much more!

People in detox don't talk very much and sleep a lot. We are in so much pain physically, mentally, and emotionally, there is no way to process the constant agony and the strong desire just to give up. We are consumed only with taking our next breath and withstanding the pain as all the substances are slowly released from our bodies. Detox is a minimum of 10 days, sometimes longer. Screams of pain and watching someone begin shaking and going into a full-blown seizure will never ever leave me, no matter how long I live. It rattles you to your core. This guy had decided he could make the transition without taking his meds. Not a good choice.

It was very eye-opening to see firsthand how many different forms of addiction there are, and the self-defeating ways victims will devise to further the disease, knowing their machinations *could* lead to death, but we all think we are going to live forever; we are immortal. *"Sometimes being a Super Hero isn't all it's cracked up to be"*. There is no treatment or recovery during detox. There is only survival.

In my case, it was difficult to read the results of my routine tests because of the meds I had to take because of my heart condition. It also took me some time before I admitted to every substance I had ingested and abused. I remember on the last two days of detox, Jimmy's face lit up with delight when the test showed I was ready for the next step. It was almost Christmas. I was missing my family, but up until this point I was just reacting to the pain, suffering, and sickness.

Believe it or not, the real challenge begins after detox. We have to learn how to function normally again because we have been forever altered. We have to remember how to be human.

"All the signs pointed to a light at the end of the tunnel, and the only question I had was, 'How long is this tunnel?' I had hit rock bottom; I was dying, and this was the last stop."

—Anthony J. Williams, III

Chapter Forty: Rehab, Phase 1, *"This was only the first week!"*

Forcing myself to relive treatment and recovery, remembering all of it in vivid

detail,

was the only way to accept the severity of dire circumstances that had brought me

here.

I was the only person who could dig myself out of an early grave. Oh, the irony of

it all...

"This is the young man who had been the sick kid who just wanted to LIVE and be

normal!"

—Anthony J. Williams, III

When I began writing my life's story, trying to come to grips with all the things I had been though, I knew this section was going to be tough. Even today knowing what I do about tucking secrets away in a special little compartment in my head and not dealing with them, I still have the tendency to want to forget the bad things. Added to this natural inclination, there's also the fact that my brain was fried from all the mind-altering chemicals I had mixed together in a rather short period of time. It would be so easy just to leave all this out, but that certainly wouldn't be honest, nor would I have learned anything from the experience. I needed to recall these events with precise clarity that resonated with the person who I had been i

order to understand "who I have become."

***

I was transferred from the "detox house" to treatment early in December
There was going to be a party that night, which everyone would be attending
"sober". Things were gearing up for the holidays even in a rehab facility. I would
find out from other patients, counselors, and doctors that the holidays are one of the
hardest times of the year to stay straight and sober. I didn't realize it then, but if
had been home, I would have celebrated Christmas and New Year's like I had every
other year since the heart surgery with plenty of alcohol, drugs, and wild times—
*"Ah, just this one last time, I can quit again after all the parties. Start next year
clean and sober; it will be easy. No problem. I know how to do this now."*

A counselor named Jeanie picked me up from the detox house and asked
about the book I had with me. I proceeded to tell her how much I was enjoying it.
It seemed like a good idea that if I was literate enough at this stage to read and
comprehend, I wasn't as bad as all the rest of the addicts. What a ruse! I had only
read the first page, and I was going to find out in my typical style, *the hard way,*
that I was just as bad as everyone else.

Jeanie and I ended up becoming life-long friends, maybe because she could
see beyond the games I was already starting to play. I was looking for the holes in
their system, thinking like I always did that I could find a better way, a faster "fix"

for me, than what they were dishing out. She got to know the *real Anthony*, the one hiding beneath the surface of charm, good looks, and witty comments. It was all an act and had been since I was a kid. To say I had been ripe for the illusion of addiction for a long time would be an understatement. The truth is that I didn't know how to live "unaltered" because I had been having a drink or a hit of something even before going to church. It really had been going on that long! But this realization would be a long time coming.

They had already determined in detox that I was a "binge" addict, what I referred to as being a "garbage disposal," mixing everything together at once. Most of the nurses in detox were recovering addicts themselves. Not sure why, but it helped to talk to someone who had been through it. This was when I was told that I would be a "recovering addict" for the rest of my life with a maintenance program in place so I could remain clean and sober. Without this, I would never have a chance at a normal life again. The addict personality was firmly in place. Every time something happened in my life, good or bad, I would crave the reward or punishment of an addictive substance. It took me quite some time to accept this because I thought I was stronger, smarter, more resilient than everybody else because of all the things I had been through.

The treatment would be in two phases, the first very structured and rigid, the second offering some freedom and responsibilities to prepare us for life back in the real world. At the beginning, I didn't know what the "real world" was supposed to be like because my "real world" had never been "normal". Gosh, I just hate how that word keeps popping up, but it's the truth!

We started with Orientation. The House Managers gave me a rundown on all the stringent rules; not all that different than living in a family atmosphere, only more regimental, I guess. They warned me about strange behavior from some of the other patients (*I thought of us all as in-mates, like in a prison or a mental institution.*) In fact, it wasn't like a prison at all, not even close, but you did have to follow all the rules; we'd be given chores to do; and of course, we had to adhere to the same strict schedule as detox.

Once I became a little acclimated, I was relieved that everyone seemed to be relatively sane; at least, at first. The stories and the cold, hard facts wouldn't become apparent until the haze had been totally lifted from my consciousness. I just had to get through each day unscathed.

I would soon notice, however, that some people had trouble with even the simplest rules, so people were always coming and going or leaving for medical reasons. This was when I experienced first-hand what it must be like for kids growing up without a loving family. They had no idea how to share, how to care, or how to respond to help. This was really foreign and frightening to me. A little *chink* in the armor towards my family was just starting to break through.

I hadn't really thought about what this was going to be like. All I had ever seen were the watered-down "made for TV" celebrity Rehabs that only report glowing successes to spark the show's ratings. The reality wasn't anywhere near as glamourous. It was downright tough, hard work. Harder than any job I have ever had, before or since.

When I would talk to people and hear their horror stories, I was drawn into a world I never knew existed. I was surprised at the men—*yes, grown men!*—who had been here multiple times. Some of them in and out of here for decades. Why would anyone put themselves through this time and time again? The pain of detox was bad enough but going through therapy and "telling all" to seasoned doctors, who knew when you weren't being truthful; you can probably imagine how difficult that was for me. I thought I could pull off the best con imaginable, but I soon learned I was just an amateur. Being a comedian just didn't cut it in here! *No one thought I was funny.*

I thought about my family, but without remorse. I would talk to them on Christmas day with the help of my therapist, but that phone call was awkward even with the doctor coaching me. I was angry for being there. It hadn't dawned on me yet what they were going through. The words "I'm sorry" and "I love you" were empty and meaningless. It would take more time for it to sink in just what I had done to them. I had none of the empathy I had felt for them during the endocarditis and especially the heart surgery. I was numb to just about everything. The counselor was helpful, but it was so early in the recovery process that I was just looking for a quick-fix and a way out of there. I was bummed out because I thought I would be home by Christmas. *Maybe by New Year's?* That was never going to happen, but no one could make me believe this so early in the program. It was mandatory for 90 days for a good reason.

***

For the first time in my life, I had to reveal my complete and utter soul. I was shocked as we worked through all the layers just how tarnished I really was. I had no idea how much resentment and anger flowed out of me. The hardest part was talking about the abuse I had suffered as a young child. I never thought I would ever tell anyone about that, but in here if I wanted to get better, I had to admit *everything!*

It was drilled into all of us the consequences of our actions if we weren't willing to make changes. Not just death as "Jimmy" had insisted was the next step for me, but the awful ways in which death would creep up on us, suffering in the most unimaginable pain, deprivation, loss of jobs, loss of family, loss of friends as everyone turned away from "the tormented addict" that no one could get through to, so everyone would be forced to give up on me.

My father's words came back to me loud and clear, *"We don't give up, Anthony. We fight; that's what we do; that's what we've always done. I'm not going to give up on you, and I don't want you to give up either!"* How could he have known? But somehow, love shows us what we need to see, even if it isn't pretty;

even if, like my dad, it's something you've never experienced before; even if love just isn't enough. *"Yeah, I thought about my folks, my sisters, and Amanda."*

***

The one line that stayed with me through all the hell I was going through was:

"Nothing changes, if nothing changes."

I add to that, "...and it only gets worse!"

This one simple sentence spoke volumes to me, and I think it will have that same effect on any person who needs to hear it. This became my new life's motto to replace the optimistic one I had so cleverly come up with in the hospital when I had been in so much pain, but surprised and motivated because I had made-it through the experimental operation of robotic surgery for someone as young as I was. It had been a last-ditch effort to save me, and I had defied the odds. Everything was looking up for me then. This was a totally different scenario. I just didn't know how someone could screw up their second, third, fourth chance at life. *How many more chances would I get?*

***

I wish I could say my story is all over now, but unfortunately, there's more to come. We've just scratched the surface of Rehab, and life isn't through yet handing me lemons. *Maybe it never will be "smooth sailing" in my life?*

Hopefully, I'm a little better prepared for what destiny has in store for me. As I mentioned earlier in this section, *"We all have to grow up and take responsibilities for our actions at some point. I just hope and pray no one waits until it's too late. I came so close to doing that, almost giving up so many times. I came so close to ending things just like Jay or Anthony Serino."*

Chapter Forty-one: Rehab, Phase 2, *"First day of the rest of my life."*

"I was introduced to the hallowed halls of Alcoholics Anonymous and Narcotics Anonymous. This was a new experience for me, and I wasn't sure I believed what they were preaching,

but I knew I only had one shot at this. I learned to "fake it until ya'make it!"

—Anthony J. Williams, III

There are so many stories I could share with my readers. Some people tried to escape and run away. I soon saw that was useless. During detox your body chemistry is going through such rapid changes that unusual psychotic episodes can result, and there were many people who were too far gone and would never make it back to reality. It left a lasting impression on me.

Right after I was transferred, an older gentleman who was having real trouble with staying sober stood at the foot of my bed and screamed *"that the house was toxic and filled with ghosts."* Unnerving, to say the least, but pulling myself together with my last ounce of strength, I told him *"to get the hell away from me!"* Thankfully, just as the words left my mouth, a counselor ran into the room and removed the man, taking him somewhere to quiet down and get help. That was what was important. I had to keep reminding myself that the people who worked in this frightening atmosphere did so to help others. I've never forgotten that. Now it is my turn to see what I can do by sharing my story to assist those tortured souls who are lost and need someone to care and understand what they're going through.

I saw the unfortunate ones who gave up on the program and left treatment, and others who needed additional medical care brought on by the ravages of time and continued heavy alcohol and drug abuse. The body and vital organs break down, which no medicine can cure. It was sad to watch this all around me, but the failure of some of those guys is probably what saved my life. Without treatment, I know I would have become just like that old man, fighting the system that was the only thing that could save him, but for him, it was probably already too late. I never saw him again.

***

"Juggling perception and reality are not something people detoxing from drugs and alcohol can do on their own. The support groups of AA and NA are for maintaining sobriety."

—Anthony J. Williams, III

My days began with a group breakfast. It was important to get used to early mornings again. Hangovers and drug withdrawal had made that a thing of the past for most of us. That's why it's so hard to hold down a job or adhere to any type of schedule. Yet, we all forget that when we're in the clutches of addiction.

We were allowed an hour in the gym after breakfast, and the rest of the day we were scheduled for multiple meetings and therapy/counselor appointments. Once a week we could pick something "fun to do", as if anything seemed like fun anymore, but it was a first step in learning to live without drugs and alcohol, which even though we'd been through detox, our bodies and minds still craved relentlessly. The first month was really rough!

It took me all of the first 30 days to start feeling better physically and for the fog to clear from my brain. Talking with other AA/NA members who had managed significant clean-and-sober time in meetings was a much-needed part of the recovery process. Listening to these people tell their personal stories really hit home with me about the damage I had done to my family and my health. I had always fought to improve my health as the "kid with the heart murmur"—everyone at school knew this—and look what I did? I went against everything and everyone I had ever learned from for a cheap thrill, *"a near comatose high!"*. I was oblivious to what I was doing, but that's no excuse. Addicts do realize there's a semblance of a problem during the *"downtime"* when we come off the drugs and booze, feeling the painful effects of needing the next binge.

I realized, in spite of myself and my ego, that you have to get right in your own head, first. You have to own up to what you did and accept the blame without putting it off on circumstances, other people, and the problems we all go through in life. We all have choices to make, and we have to own up to the bad decisions we make as well as our achievements. It's a balancing act, but a necessary one. Without this recognition within ourselves, there is no going forward.

We also had to accept that not everyone is going to forgive us for our actions. There is no fresh start. We have to live with the past, but the more time you're sober, the better your future decision-making process will become. That's the only thing that we, as individuals, can control.

All of these valuable lessons were introduced to us during the first 30 days. It would take another 60 days to accept them in totality, instead of just lip-service trying to convince the counselors and doctors that we were *"cured"*, when in actuality we were just playing a role that we thought was expected of us. *"How do doctors, therapists, and counselors know the difference? They have clues, I guess, but they never really know for sure. Hence, the number of repeat addicts coming back for treatment."*

Right after the holidays, my first 30 days, there was a significant event in my own life that saddened and humbled me, but perhaps it helped me to accept my own behavior. It certainly woke me up to reality. To this point, the only family members that knew about me and "A Better Tomorrow" were my parents and sisters. When I wasn't there for Christmas Day or New Year's Day, the time for the extended family and my friends to know what was going on had to be addressed. Everyone suspected that some kind of problem had been brewing with me for a while because there had been other holidays when I hadn't shown up because I was on a "binge" or recovering from one.

My whole family was at my grandparents' home for Christmas, and I made the decision to tell them myself. I felt I had dealt with enough pain and I needed a release. I needed to know where I stood with the rest of the family, especially my grandparents. They would either accept me or reject me. I consulted my therapist, who was supportive of my decision, telling me it would truly begin the healing process. I agonized over whether I'd really be able to do it when the time came. I had so many doubts. The therapist and I talked about what would be my responsibilities and what couldn't be mine. I couldn't stop them from having their own opinions or change what they might say. I could only be honest and tell them about my addictions, the rehab, and accept their reactions. This was the hardest thing I had ever had to do in my whole life!

I called on the phone to wish everyone a Merry Christmas. The line went completely silent as I confessed that I was in Rehab doing everything I could do to correct my addictive behavior. I could hear someone sniffling in tears in the background. After I got it all out, I expected that they would hate me forever. I couldn't believe it when all I heard was encouragement, support, and how proud of me they were. My grandfather told me, "It took a lot of courage for you to do this yourself." His words gave me the strength to continue, to accept my blame, and to stick with it.

After climbing the mountain of the first 30 days from hell, my life started to fall into place. I would be working with a sponsor after the program ended. His name was Leo, and he was from New York. He is still a dear friend, whom I hold in the highest regard. We started with the AA/NA 12-step program. I knew I had nowhere else to go, no job, no future plans. The real work didn't start until the 90 day recovery was over.

The first 30 days, in essence, were a cleanse for me, but not everyone is that fortunate. 90 days provides the best chance for a longer-term recovery. Accepting that it's never going to go away, and that I will always be in a permanent recovery period for the rest of my life was the hardest thing for me to understand, but this final truth is the most important lesson to grasp. When life and its balancing act of good things and bad steps back in with strong emotions of fear, anxiety, depression, compulsiveness, as well as all the beautiful things we experience in life, we have to find a way to compensate and react. Being involved in your own recovery is the only way to make this happen. My view of the world and everything in it had changed for me. Drugs and alcohol are no longer my first thought in the morning and the last thing on my mind when I go to sleep at night. My feelings of "what can I do for me" have changed to "how can I help you".

This process was put into place about a decade ago, but it wasn't until I decided to piece together my life story for my own support a year ago that I realized that maybe my story could help other people find themselves, as I had to do, and have the desire to live again. As an addict, you really don't care whether you live or die. It's all about the next "binge", the next "high", the next "thrill".

After I ended the 90-day recovery and while still working on my 12-step program, I decided to stay with a friend in California. This was a friend I had met in treatment. I had become close with him and his family. I'm sure my parents would have preferred for me to come home, but all my support groups, sponsor, new friends were here. Besides the warm weather and palm trees appealed to me.

This begins a new saga in my life;

"Maybe, just maybe, I was where I was supposed to be!"

SECTION X

Different Place and Surroundings; Same Old Me.

"Could I remain this healed 'me' for the rest of my life?"

Chapter Forty-two: Alone in California, *"Where would I go now?"*

"A little rebellion near the end of Phase 1, Rehab, gave me much needed clarity and hope!"

—Anthony J. Williams, III

The rebel in me will never completely disappear, but the stubborn, rebellious part of my nature has always given me the strength to overcome obstacles that most people my age have never had to face. Herein, I believe, lies my fortitude. I desperately needed it more at this time in my life than any other to "reinvent" the new, improved, more mature *Anthony J. Williams, III.* I really can thank my dad, especially, but my whole family as well for believing in me and not crushing this *Super-Hero* spirit. It is how I have survived and thrived, even when it felt like the world was falling apart. I knew *proving myself to my family* would be the biggest challenge to face in the near future.

Yet, regardless, I decided to *"test the rules in Rehab"* because I thought I could. My ego was still very much alive and well. In fact, as my confidence in myself grew, the unique parts of my personality returned, but I like to think in a much more positive manner.

While attending meetings, I met a cute girl, Amber, who was actually the daughter of a friend who was in treatment with me. She'd given me her phone number, and we talked during "phone time" which was approved for a short period in the evening. The more interested I became in Amber, the more I wanted a normal sequence of events. *Ya'know, like a date? Like in real life? Wasn't that what Phase 2 was supposed to be all about? But I hadn't quite made it to Phase 2 yet.*

I managed to convince her to meet me around the corner from the facility, late at night when everyone else was asleep. I had no intention of running away. I just wanted a little free time to be with a young, attractive girl who understood what I was going through. I wanted to be the same charming Anthony I had always been without having to be drunk, stoned, and then just falling into bed with whomever I happened to be with, which of course had a huge part in the breakup of my engagement. I knew there was no going back to Amanda, even though I would always be grateful to her for what she taught me about love and commitment. This was more innocent, like high school dating, or in my case maybe junior high school dating. I wanted to relive a happier time before the pressures and drama of sickness, surgery, and addiction had taken over my life.

Amber and I met around the corner, sat and talked, listening to music and having a few laughs. Nothing intimate happened, we just *"chilled and chatted"*. This was the first time in quite a few years that I'd experienced a healthy interaction with another human being, especially of the opposite sex, when I wasn't trying to *"score"*. Not just in a sexual sense; "dates" were to consume whatever liquor and drugs a female addict had to share. *"It was how the game was played."*

After Amber drove off that night, I was able to sneak back into my room without disturbing anyone or getting caught. The best feeling was the next morning when I woke up with a smile on my face with no urge for drink, drugs, or meaningless sex. All I wanted was more freedom!

One of the patients must have heard or seen me come back to the facility and turned me into the house manager. The penalty for this delayed me from entering Phase 2 of the program another week. I was pissed about it because I really hadn't done anything wrong; in my opinion, I had done something *right!* I had proven to myself that I could be out on my own without craving or even thinking about my previous addictions. But we all know we have to pay the piper when we go off on our own. They also informed my parents that I had gotten into trouble. I certainly didn't need that either, but I like to think that Amber and I both benefited from our first date.

When I left rehab to stay with my friend Dana, it was Amber who came and picked me up. We ended up dating and supporting each other through this delicate transition in both of our lives. She was also really helpful in helping me work out the insecurities I had about my family.

***

"There was nothing I believed to be more valuable than my sobriety."

I felt like I was letting my folks down by not coming back home, but they assured me they agreed with my decision to stay in my current support group, which was working out really well; my sponsor, Leo; and Dana's family who had willingly offered to take me in until we could get our own place. When I'd made this choice, I didn't know how I was going to get my car, clothes, and personal belongings from the east coast to the west coast, roughly 3000 miles. I was starting all over again with nothing, but I wanted things to be different from what had brought me here.

I just couldn't risk falling back into the group of friends and coworkers who had shown me a "lifestyle" that almost ended my life. This meant giving up the Real Estate business as well. It was my own fault. I had made these decisions, but the environment had been toxic for all of us.

Jay's death from overdosing hit me harder after rehab than it ever had before. After the initial collapse while on the phone with Jay's brother, I let myself become numb through substance abuse. It allowed me to not experience the grief that I still had to deal with; another reason not to go back to New York. So many memories of how badly I'd treated people and old friends were continuing to surface. The real recovery isn't over with a certificate from a Rehab Center; in truth, it was all just beginning.

I had to face how I had left things back in New York regarding my torn and tattered past. It was safe to assume the jobs I had held were gone. In California, I would need to find a job, get transportation worked out, and have the right clothes to present myself clean, sober, and professional for interviews and building a new career path. Life didn't miraculously start again after rehab; it became a series of worrisome adult resolutions. This is what "A Better Tomorrow" had been trying to prepare us for, but it only sinks in when you find yourself all alone with lots of choices to make on a whole new level with no crutch of addiction to dilute the urgency and fear.

Mom sent me out a few boxes of clothes, including outfits that were suitable for the job market. She sent everything I asked for, including shoes, hats, and some of the personal items that had given me stability. Things I used to do before my mind and emotions had been clogged with poison. I was fortunate. I had some really great support. I had a regular schedule of meetings which I attended religiously, a girlfriend that supported my sobriety, sober friends, and the support of my family back home. I was surprised to find that I had new-found confidence that had been missing from my life for years—probably all the way back to when I'd failed at the university and hockey.

There was one more surprise being set up that I didn't know about, which would prove to be my saving grace through this difficult transition. My parents called to make sure I had received all the boxes and packages they had sent me.

They told me they were going to make a cross-country trip to bring my car out to California *and just as importantly to see me*. I was so shocked! They were going to attempt it without stopping along the way so they could spend as much time with me as possible. Until the tears of happiness poured down my face, I hadn't allowed myself to reach deep within and feel the loss of being without my family. This wasn't just "my" life anymore. I had help; I had support; I had dear people who were in my corner. I knew I would never let anyone down again. I decided then and there it would be my future to help others as was done for me.

"The biggest blessing that was robbed from me by addiction was the simple conversations with loved ones, my family and friends, who had always been there for me.

I had been too blind to see, but suddenly my eyes were opened!"

Chapter Forty-three: Reinvent "Me" to Rebuild My Life, *"Stability?"*

There is a saying, "When the rubber hits the road..."
In my simplest terms, I interpret it as, "LIFE IS HARD!"

—Anthony J. Williams, II

I know and appreciate how fortunate I was to have my loving family and friends, who stood by me, in spite of all the trouble I got myself into and the difficul health issues I'd faced my entire life. I also know there are many people who don' have any support system at all. Does that make this process even harder? *"Yes, believe it does, in a way."* But, at the end of the day when you recap what transpire within your own mind, everyone is alone with the decisions they've made, th scattered thoughts that seem to go nowhere, and the extreme conflict of emotior ***"Stability"*** seemed like the highest rung on the ladder to reach, and I kept missin it.

The next two years of my life were spent within my own conscienc working on myself. There were many anxious moments, but thankfully, there wei quite a few good moments too. Those are the brief interludes which strengthen t to get over the next hurdle or keep going on the AA/NA 12-Step Program.

I had completed the first 5 steps while still in Rehab, but it's so easy to ditch the rest when the cold, cruel world creeps back into reality. That's why, even though I've said it numerous times already, I encourage everyone to stick to the program and continue going to the meetings, work with a sponsor, and *never, ever* think that you can do it by skipping steps or all by yourself. The social aspects of speaking and listening to other members and supporting them as well is so necessary. We're at different stages on the path of the continuous journey, and we all have something to give, as well as something to take-away, from every single meeting.

Right around the 6-month sobriety mark, I realized I wasn't thinking about getting drunk or using anymore. It's almost funny how these breakthroughs sneak up on you. It takes one of these milestone markers and the reflection it creates to see how far you've come, but also how much work you still have to do.

I think the hardest thing for me was to silence my own mind. I kept rehashing the poor decisions I'd made, the people I'd let down, the missed opportunities I'd squandered, and all the time I'd wasted. It's almost impossible to move forward without getting stuck in the past because "the past" is all we know for sure. No one can predict what will happen tomorrow.

Being in California was good for me, but I really did miss New York and being able to lean on my family whenever I needed it. Yet, I had to face these demons on my own so as not to fall back into the trap that had destroyed my life in he first place. My first priority was that I had to get a job to support the "new, reinvented me".

I fell back on my basic straightforward and blunt personality traits. I'd always been this way. Some people can find me difficult to deal with when I'm being stubborn and obnoxious, but I didn't really care. I also found that I met some really good people and made friends with strong- willed individuals like myself or those who were encouraged by my *"tough-love"*.

One of the first things I did was contact my ex-girlfriend in New York—we hadn't talked since that brief phone call on the way to the facility. I had made the decision that I was staying here in California, and I needed to let her know. It was another difficult phone call, but afterwards, I felt a sense of doing things the right way. The distance between us was a big help in the sadness that surfaced. I also had a full-time girlfriend, Amber, which eased the pain of separation.

I decided that I needed to do everything totally different from what I had done before. I took a job as a "Repo Man". It was a start. I needed to stay busy, go to meetings, and move forward.

"A wandering mind is a dangerous thing for a recovering addict/alcoholic."

***

Shortly after receiving my 1-year sobriety chip, I knew I had to start making more permanent, critical decisions. The feeling of fulfillment is a powerful motivator for me. I had made it a full year. That first year I was marking-time getting-my-feet-wet, surviving. Now I needed to make definite plans for the future. It conjured up memories of living only for my dream of playing professional hockey which followed me all through school. Acceptance is critical for me, and the recognition of another significant evolution took hold of me. *"Yes, it was time…"* I ended the relationship with Amber, my rehab girlfriend. I just couldn't think of her as anything else. This young woman did so much for me, and I will always be grateful. She accepted me, loved me, and helped me understand that my life was worth more than drugs and cheap booze. Unfortunately, we were both going through a raw transition which created different types of immaturity in both of us. The breakup was inevitable, but it still hurt like hell. Another part of my life where I had failed, but there had been other relationships I had ended and questioned. Too often, I overstayed my welcome in love. What I thought was "love" was tainted by the past. The 12 Steps allowed me to accept love without the fear of physical abuse which I had suffered as a child.

"Putting the pain aside meant there had been growth.

Working though the Twelve Steps of Alcoholics Anonymous had brought me

peace."

Testimonial by Ronnie

I meant Anthony, or Tony, as I call him, through a group of friends who also fondly refer to him as Tony. Although I don't remember the exact moment we met, I remember hearing stories about him leading up to and prior to meeting him. All were stories of great times and memories, mostly fun and funny. Once I met him, I instantly saw what everyone was talking about. His personality, charm, wit, sense of humor, all matched what I had heard. Being a gay man who had recently came out not long after meeting Tony, when meeting new people, it could be a bit intimidating to decide if it's something you tell people you have just meet or not. I don't remember the exact words coming out of my mouth, but I remember being able to be myself around Tony and not have any criticism or judgment to worry about. He accepted me as I was, made me feel comfortable in my own skin, and to this day we continue to have fun and joke about things because that's the kind of relationship we built. He is a true, committed friend. The last time he came to NY I was not able to attend the BBQ our group was having for him because I had to work. He messaged me and asked if he could come to my job and visit me, and I of course said yes. Tony kept his word and went out of his way to come visit me at work and that meant a lot in a time where a lot of people say things and don't follow through. Tony followed through. I met Tony at a time in his life when he had many struggles. But in all honesty, who doesn't have struggles? It's the actions you take to move in a better direction and to better yourself and that's what Tony did when he moved away from NY. We were sad to see him go but knew that the move was what he had to do. He now has a beautiful family and has greatly improved himself. Our group still keeps in touch with him, whether it be from social media, FaceTiming, etc, and every time we go through pictures from the past and we see Tony, we all smile. He might live across the country, but he is always going to be a part of "the group".

Chapter Forty-four: Relationships, *"Why did this keep happening?"*

We all have different types of "relationships" with a myriad of people. In my case: girlfriends, friends, my parents and sisters, other family members, coworkers, and even casual acquaintances. These interactions show us how we are perceived by others, even if we don't always agree with the vague, subliminal messages that are hidden behind empty smiles or mirthless laughter. How do you know when someone is being sincere or just giving you a line?

The answer is, *"you don't know"*. It makes it hard to get an accurate take on where you're really at in the grand scheme of things, and I've always wondered if my impressions were merely shadows lost in the recesses of my mind, stuck between the soul and my strong ego.

While I was recovering from addiction, I thought I'd be content being alone for the rest of my life, focusing on the work I needed to do to correct all the damage I had done to my family. I felt I wasn't adequate for a genuine, heartfelt relationship and feared this might always be the case. Leo, my sponsor, and I had talked about this before. I had confided in him about the abuse that I had buried deep inside me so far that even I could forget about it at times. I also thought we'd made substantial breakthroughs, and it was gone forever. Yet, here I was; another relationship had gone down in flames, and the thought of rushing back into another one was out of the question. The secrets seemed to have everlasting roots which were growing again to the point of resurfacing.

I went to Leo, knowing I needed to tell him everything or my tentative peace would crash-and-burn as well. I remember after unburdening myself about Amber and our relationship, I told him I was sorry. It's amazing how the right words at just the right time can break through barriers that we didn't even know existed. Leo looked me straight in the eye and in one sentence—*"You don't need to apologize…"*—he helped fix the completely broken "me" and restore the "me" that I always should have been. I had been apologizing my entire life for the time when I didn't speak up, didn't trust enough to ask for help, and I saw all the prior relationships that I didn't respect enough because I didn't respect myself enough. Living in California, just out of Rehab with the clutches of addiction still wanting to devour me, I was suddenly free from all judgment. This baggage had been pulling me down for over 15 years!

My family didn't know anything about this yet, and it was way too heavy of a topic to approach them with right now, but times were changing and letting go of this burden, which truly had never been my own in the first place, would give me the strength to cling to my new friends and sponsor as I vowed to be the best erson I could be for what I had to offer. At this point, I had no idea what I had left o offer, but at least now, maybe I could find out.

***

"Years of drug use and alcohol abuse, mixed with depression and a feeling of inadequacy,

doesn't provide the best tools for paving a career path that leads to a solid future."

—Anthony J. Williams, III

Dana and I finally got our small, two-bedroom apartment, splitting the rent and other expenses in half. It was a way for us both to help each other with our continued rehabilitation and keep track of our AA/NA meetings with a little more privacy than what we had with his family. We may have been acting like teenagers in many ways, but we were grown men in our early-to-mid-twenties, and it was time to leave childhood and dependence on family and addictive substances behind. *Talk about not having "the best tools" for professional development in the job-market; we had no skills! All we had were haunting memories and the fear of messing up again.*

My relationship with Amber, my rehab girlfriend, would eventually push Dana out of the apartment. It was just too difficult for two guys in a tiny apartment to co-exist when only one of them is in a relationship. Amber and I were having difficulties as well, which I'm sure didn't help. There were heated arguments between her and me, and everything was just too close-for-comfort.

I also gave up the Repo job even though it had the potential for me to make a decent living, and Dana and I had a few laughs over funny stories from the job. I just didn't have much of a career future. A buddy of mine owned his own carpentry business that handled government contracts, so there was always plenty of work. It wasn't the best job, again no upward progression, but it kept me busy and out of trouble.

After a while I got another room-mate, but I found out he was smoking crack and even stole money from me. He was an addict, for sure. Not at all what I needed to be around. It was a great reminder, however, of what life used to be like back in New York when I had to stash drugs and related paraphernalia whenever anyone was coming over for a visit.

It was a jolt at first to remember these addictive behaviors, but my happy-go-luck personality found an ounce of relief and a lot of freedom in not having that hanging over my head anymore. *"Anybody could stop by anytime they wanted,"* I smiled to myself, tongue-in-cheek.

The realization that I had nothing to hide was beneficial because my parents and I were traveling to-and-from New York to California to see each other as much as possible. I also had, and still have, dear supportive friends in New York that I need to see. They've been such a help in this ongoing, grueling, recovery process. When I go into a slump and start remembering all the ugly things from my addict years, some of which I'm still digging out of my psyche even now, they're always there for me, just a phone call away. They know me and can talk me down off that ledge that continues to creep up on me at the worst possible times; sometimes, for no reason at all.

All of this helped my sobriety and plans for the future. It was a big learning step for my own growth and self-worth. Other people, even family members, were beginning to notice my late-blooming maturity. Relationships, however, were definitely something I needed to work on.

After the problem with the second room-mate, I moved into a friend's house, Christy. She became like an older sister to me. After all, I was used to having older sisters to look up to—Michelle and Tara. Little did I know that right after I made this move, there was a big shift on the horizon that would test me, encourage me, and teach me the only way that I can be taught … *the school of experience and hard knocks that turned into my dreams for "a better tomorrow"*.

Chapter Forty-five: Getting Back Out There, *"How else do you do it?"*

After Amber and I split up, I was on my own for almost a year, working on myself with my sponsor Leo and other friends I had made at the meetings. Yeah, there were those who came and went on an irregular basis and, sadly, some who *"fell off the wagon"* and never returned. We always wondered what happened to them. We talked about it. Tried to get in touch with them. Offered our help, but many times to no avail.

Someone might resurface months or even years later, starting all over at the beginning and showing signs of devastating health issues, mental and emotional breakdowns, and heightened addict behavioral issues that were just too painful to watch. We tried to support them even more because we all knew if they started drinking or abusing drugs again, it could well be their last. Death is the shadow that follows the recurring addict for the rest of their lives. Yet, some people just couldn't stay "clean". It reinforced in me my desire not to be a victim again. I felt like I had always been a victim. I had to break the pattern of self-pity which had led to my anger and losing faith in my family, my friends, and my life. We are only a victim if we let ourselves become one.

With an addict, there is no way to filter out the raw feelings and haunting memories that will keep overwhelming us. I was now almost two years beyond the institutional intervention. There is no set timeline on how long it's going to take or how many times the desire for alcohol and drugs will return, cropping up when we least expect it. I found that as long as I continued fighting and working towards an internal peace, I could stick with the plan.

"Recovery from addiction is not a sprint, but rather a marathon.

Many water-break stops on the run which could turn into mistakes, but I

learned from them,

turned out to be the blessing I needed for the next chapter of my life.

—Anthony J. Williams, III

***

I continued to go to all of the AA meetings after I moved out of the apartment. I stayed close enough so that I didn't have to change sponsors—Leo's advice and friendship was the best thing that had ever happened to me!—and I didn't want to switch locations for the meetings, either. My support system and friends were in place, and I didn't want to mess things up again.

I was still very emotionally vulnerable. I knew I had a fear of relationships but I didn't really talk about it. I had plenty of other upsetting memories to sort through, so I just let past romantic attachments smolder in the background of my mind with no idea of what the future would bring. I wouldn't let myself think about it. I felt that I was too damaged to reach out to anyone.

Things happen so many times with no forethought or planning. One night, after a meeting, I was standing outside with some buddies of mine just talking and joking around. I noticed this girl walking towards me. I had seen her before and knew who she was, of course, but I never really thought anything about it.

I'll never forget the moment she came right up to me and said, "I think you're cute." Acting like *Mr. Cool* who was used to this sort of thing happening all the time, I just smiled and said, "Thank you." She smiled back and continued on her way to her own car. Stunned by her remark, I just watched her walk away.

The friend I was standing next to turned to me and said, "Are you going to let that go?"

I wasn't sure what to do, but I couldn't look like an idiot in front of my pals. So, I just reacted or "acted out the part", pretending I knew exactly what I was doing. My stomach was in knots when I came up beside her next to the car.

I was still getting used to this new, clean, sober life, and things seemed to be heading in the right direction. Would something like this create a problem? I didn't realize how immature I was being, thinking that just talking to a woman would disrupt my whole equilibrium. There was no guarantee it would develop into a relationship.

I was totally over-reacting, but that's when it hit me that what I wanted the most out of life—love—was what scared me the most! I was terrified of being rejected or have someone fall out of love with me because I didn't understand how be in a serious relationship. I was lost! And I knew it was all my fault because I really didn't "know what to do!"

My past had finally caught up to me and was playing games with my head. don't even remember exactly what I said to her when I came up beside her, but she smiled warmly back at me, and somehow, we agreed to "hang out some time."

This was the first time in a long time, over two years, where I was taking a chance on life and thinking about a future. All of the sudden, everything seemed to have a reason. I had been living just day-to-day for so long, anything planned for tomorrow just didn't exist. I was doing something not based on the current moment or the only option available, I was agreeing to something beyond the minute-by-minute structure that had been keeping me sane after my whole life had fallen apart. I had totally forgotten what this felt like. Yeah, I was scared, but it felt kind of good too. *Was I ready? Only one way to find out!*

"At that moment in time, I never could have dreamed that one quick

decision

would alter my reality … FOREVER!"

—Anthony J. Williams, III

SECTION XI

<u>The Time had Come for Me to Grow Up.</u>

"The best news was an 'Oops'! How would I

cope?"

Chapter Forty-six: A Chance at a Relationship, *"Could it be love?"*

"Who was I to know what love was when all I ever planned was getting the next fix?

Like the movie "Groundhog's Day", repeating the same thing day after day. Good way to describe addiction and definition of insanity when you expect different results."

—*Guilty as charged,* Anthony J. Williams, III

The start of a new life started with that first date with the girl from the parking lot, *Kendyl.* I felt so unworthy, but it was comfortable because we were *"just going to hang out; friends, right?"* I had absolutely nothing with which to impress her—no fancy new car, still using the 2000 Nissan Maxima my parents had driven out from New York for me a couple of years before. I was trying to save some money, but I certainly didn't have much of a bank account. I was a recovering addict with a mechanical valve in my heart; why would anyone want to be with me?

She seemed to want to get to know me. She was tall, beautiful, and exuded confidence. Every time we hung out, it just felt natural. She was so easy to be with. She didn't seem to care about hot cars and lots of money in the bank. She just wanted me to spend time with her, and I had plenty of time to give. We hit it off right away. I didn't know much about a successful relationship, but I knew right away that it was love. I had some anxious moments wondering if she felt it too.

The day burnt into my memory for all eternity and my life-changing moment, which gave me something *real* to live for, was being asleep on the couch and waking up to Kendyl sitting right on top of me. She was staring down at me intently and said, "You know I love you, right?"

Like an idiot, through the fog of sleep, I answered, "What did I do?" I had to have done something wrong. It had to be my fault, and a girl like her must be upset to feel anything for a guy like me. My guilty conscious from all of my failed past relationships was rearing its ugly head.

She continued talking to me and told me what I did; we did—she was pregnant. My world seemed to shrink. We were the only two people that mattered anymore. I said softly, "Okay."

I didn't know what else to say. I'd never been through a conversation like this before. Mono syllables were all I could handle. *Hey, I was scared, confused, but excited at the same time. We weren't the only two people involved in this; there was one more—a baby!*

Kendyl was surprised that I was so calm. I guess, she expected me to be angry or upset. My life was wide awake and moving rapidly forward. I needed some advice. The person I trusted the most was my dad. My excitement was already starting to build.

I didn't even wait for confirmation from the doctor. My folks were just getting ready to go out with friends when I called to tell them they were going to be grandparents again. There was a hesitant pause, then "the talk" with my dad. First thing he said was, "Anthony, do the right thing."

That was all I needed to hear. It was time for me to grow up and face the music. I needed to attend to my responsibilities. This was a rather unconventional way to share the news with family, but when had I ever done anything the conventional way? Another zinger and huge change in the life of Anthony Williams, but it just made sense. Kendyl and I shared common core values, even though we're very different in regard to our interests, but that keeps life interesting, right? We decided immediately that we were getting married.

Both of us having gone through addiction and recovery knew how tentative life could be, and we were going to be bringing a new *"life"* into the world. Not all of our friends and family agreed, but it was our decision. Some of the friends from AA were actually taking bets on how long *"we"* would last. It was sad to hear that some people didn't think we'd make it even 90 days.

It wasn't easy; we've had challenges, which I will share with you, but going from "addicts to a family" was one of the best decisions we have made together. I was an "oops!", but the best thing that could have happened. Our lives weren't just our own anymore. We were having a baby!

Chapter Forty-seven: From Addicts to Marriage, *"Were we crazy?"*

"I went from wanting to commit suicide to shopping at Babies 'R' Us.

Our lives couldn't have been turned more upside down,

but we were both open-minded, willing, and able to adapt to this decision.

We realized for the first time since our recovery just what acceptance truly

meant."

—Anthony J. Williams, III, and the future Mrs. Kendyl Williams

We were married in a church in Temecula, California, by a Pastor Dominick. We met with him prior to the ceremony, and he helped us to understand that we had a long road ahead of us. We shared with the pastor our story of meeting after an AA meeting and that we both were newly recovering alcoholics/addicts. It brought the excitement down a notch to be warned by a member of the clergy that this wasn't going to be easy. But he agreed to do the ceremony, so in his own way, he was putting his faith in us, just as we were putting our faith in him and our future.

The wedding itself was anti-climatic. There weren't very many people there. Our families from the east coast weren't able to travel cross-country for the wedding. There was a reception in a friend's backyard with about 25 people in attendance. I don't think we're even in contact with most of those people, now that time and separation onto different life paths has intervened.

The plan from the beginning, however, had been to go to the east coast for a large reception with our families, and we stuck to that plan. This definitely made up for the lackluster wedding in California. We will always be grateful to Pastor Dominick. He gave us the straight scoop on what to expect in married life and blessed us in spite of his own genuine concern that this was going to be difficult. A baby on the way complicated matters, of course, as it would for any couple.

The reception in New York was everything we could have wanted, and the first time that most of my family would be meeting Kendyl. She was beautiful, respectful, and wonderful to everyone. I was so proud to be by her side. *Maybe I had finally done something right!*

I had been apprehensive about seeing cousins, grandparents, and friends since this was the first time many had seen "me" since I'd left New York for treatment. It all went so well, though. The time spent in New York *"brought home"* the meaning of family. Having Kendyl with me made everything feel right. I hadn't felt *"right"* about anything in a long time. This motivated me even more to start building a new life, a new future, and be the best father I could be. *Look what a great role model I had in my own parents!* It takes two people working together like my own mom and dad had done. My father worked hard so that mom could be home with me and my sisters.

Being with Kendyl's family was just as eye-opening. I could see that they had solid family values, which had shaped Kendyl into the incredible woman she had become, even after going through a rough time in life, just as I was. Now it was time to let go of the past and create a beginning for us as a family. The baby, still months away from being born, became *so real to me!*

The flight back to California after all the support from our families was bittersweet. It was so wonderful to have been with everyone, but sad that our families were so far away. We knew the time ahead was going to be *"all on us"*. We had to deal with the pregnancy, the birth of our child, and learn how to be parents on our own. It really was a big change. Pastor Dominick had not minced words. We would think of him often, as well our families, when our lives were altering in some small or large fashion every single day.

I remember the day that we found out the sex of the baby. Kendyl's family knew the doctor who would be delivering our baby. He would joke around with us during her checkups. This really helped put us at ease. A close friend had joined us for this monumental appointment. When I found out that we were having a son, the excitement really hit us both! There was no turning back, and we were very happy. I realized I was finally accepting responsibility for my actions. If ever there was a definition for a boy becoming a man, this would be how I would define it.

"It was surreal how life could change so drastically in such a short time.

How does a person like me with so many problems receive the blessing of a baby boy?"

—Anthony J. Williams, III

***

Time flew by so quickly. Before we knew what hit us, we were on-call for the baby to be born. There were so many preparations to handle. The first scare that our little one was coming into this world turned out to be a false alarm. I was disappointed that we had to go back home and wait. I had been so overjoyed!

I can't tell you what Kendyl was going through. She must have been terrified! And I didn't like seeing her in pain. She was the one giving birth, and the baby would be totally dependent on her for quite some time. But fathers are necessary too, even at the very beginning. Especially when the next time she started having pains, it was the real thing; no false alarm this time!

"AJ" entered our lives at 8 lbs, 10 ounces; perfectly healthy. Kendyl was tired but glowing radiantly. I loved her so much! It relieved me to see him so perfect because I couldn't help but think about the health problems I had as an infant. I instantly felt a quiver and knew it was love for a baby that I never dreamed could be so strong, but I also felt an immediate sense of protectiveness, responsibility, and accountability. I was proud. I was happy. I was scared!

Taking him home from the hospital dampened our euphoria. Both Kendyl and I were full of fear and totally exhausted. She was on maternity leave, but she would have to go back to work. I was saving all the money I could, but there are tons of expenses with a baby on the way.

I had been doing some research on careers because I knew I had to provide better for my family. I really didn't want Kendyl to have to go back to work, but right now, there was just no other option. I also wanted a career with not only a future, but something I would really enjoy doing, something I could be proud of and would intrigue my mind. Since living in California, I had only taken whatever job was thrown my way to keep my head above water while I was recovering. It was time for that to stop now. Time to grow up and plan for the future of my family.

The idea of going to school for Game Design was a real interest. Video games had gotten me through so many horrible times during my childhood and teenage years. I met with the school and crunched some numbers, but it just wasn't doable. I realized for the first time since high school that I had *"another dream"* besides hockey. Something I really wanted and knew that I could do. I wanted to help others have the same experiences that had saved me when my health was taken away from me with endocarditis and a failing heart valve. Also, it had forged life long friendships.

I knew this would have to wait, however, because parenthood and inexperience was taking a toll on our love, our marriage. We were doing whatever we could to make ends meet and make sure AJ had everything he needed. At the same time, we were still attending AA meetings. That turned out to be a blessing in disguise, however, and time well spent when I became reacquainted with a person who had made such a huge difference in my recovery during rehab. She was the director of the intake department. She offered me an opportunity to help others at the same facility where I had been, "A Better Tomorrow". It seemed like a perfect fit and the answer to our prayers.

My life seems to have always been filled with opposite polarities. I went from needing help as a drug addict and alcoholic to someone giving help to guys who were in the same boat. The first couple of phone calls I made to suffering addicts and their families brought back so many disturbing memories. It showed me what my family had gone through getting me into the program.

I was consulting with families, just like my own, in hopes of getting an addict into treatment because the next phone call might be to notify them of their loved one's death. But the high ideals that I had for this were rapidly fading away as the facility became corporate-owned. Somehow the corporate-structure mentality of the times made all the morals that I had adhered to and been re-instructed in since my childhood a thing of the past. The lady who hired me who had such high hopes was fired. There was no place left for us in this type of climate. We didn't fit in anymore.

The plans for getting a degree in Game Design was put back in motion, even though our marriage was definitely on the rocks. We just couldn't deal with all the pressure in our lives. Kendyl had a job with benefits, but it would be stressful for me to be home all the time going to school. We would have to make mega changes in our lives, and we didn't know where to start.

We attended a class to learn about love languages, only to find out we weren't even on the same page. We met another couple there, Andy and Nancy. They were going through similar problems and not coping any better than we were. It seemed like each time we broke through one barrier another obstacle would take its place. Each hurdle got tougher and larger. It just seemed like we were doing everything wrong, which I took to mean "I WAS DOING EVERYTHING WRONG!" I know it takes two to do things right or wrong, but I was putting all the blame on myself. I returned to my previous feeling of being a victim and that things just weren't fair.

We tried marriage counseling with various therapists, but that only seemed to cause more resentment between us. Both of us had the keys to unlock the wonderful relationship we'd had initially, but we just didn't know how or when to use them. So, in spite of all the animosity and confusion between us, me going back to school seemed like a selfish act on my part, but it turned out to be the only answer that made sense. I knew this would either make or break my marriage, but I had to give it a try. We needed a drastic change to stop the misery which had engulfed us.

Full-Sail University located in Winter Park, Florida, offered an online Game Design program. I decided this was the degree that I needed in order to be successful in this career. It had quite a bit of flexibility, so I could pick and chose what I really wanted to excel in. Being online was also the only way I could work this into our conflicting lives.

Kendyl was working the least number of hours possible to keep our insurance benefits. I took a job in sales to augment our income while going to school online. The bills were getting paid, but it was tearing our relationship to shreds. This seemed like a haunting echo from the past relationship failures I had known my whole life. I was at home during the day, taking care of AJ.

It was only a matter of time before everything started to fall apart. We decided it was best for us to have some time apart because our home was getting toxic, which would affect not only us, but AJ as well. Kendyl went to stay with her parents. We shared our time with AJ and agreed not to fight in front of him. It was hard for me not to say the things that cropped up in my mind when things just weren't working, but we both tried for our son's sake. Divorce wasn't being discussed or considered, but we knew we had to slow things down or there would be no going back. Her staying with her folks was a sad and hard decision, but it was for the best. We talked to the couple from the first class, Andy and Nancy. They were shocked to hear that we had actually separated. We had some decisions to make that couldn't be done with the tension between us. We had to be on our own or divorce would have to be considered. I didn't want to fail again.

"Asking the tough questions and being confident in our answers to each

other

was the only way we could start to move forward again. If that was even

possible…

It was like someone had lit a match and ignited gasoline to destroy our

marriage."

Chapter Forty-eight: Parenthood is Survival, *"Did I know that? No."*

"As new parents, you can use all the help and advice you can get. It's scary!
Kids don't exactly come with instruction manuals.
And here we were, separated, being both mom and dad to AJ without each other."

—Anthony J. Williams, III

Since I was fired from my last job as an assistant at the rehab facility, as well as almost everybody else, it resulted in a class-action suit which provided enough money to support us for a short time. Since I was basically making decisions on my own, finishing school and getting my degree seemed to me to be the only way to comfortably take care of my family. I never thought of having to just take care of myself. I refused to accept that our marriage was over. I loved Kendyl and she loved me, even when we couldn't agree on anything except our love for our son. It was our common ground and a blessing, no matter how volatile our marriage had become.

Honest communication was stifled or nonexistent for quite a while, but once we grew tired of the silence, we realized we had to share our sincere feelings with each other. It took a level of maturity that neither of us realized we hadn't reached yet. As parents, we thought we were adults, when we really weren't. *"In the early days of our marriage and right after AJ was born, we had been merely playing house."*

The little bit of money, however, eased things enough so that Kendyl and I could look at our situation more realistically. We had to quit playing games with each other and get serious about how we could put things back together as a family. It took a lot of effort for both of us, but at the end of the day and especially at the end of the lonely weekends, we knew we still loved each other, even if we had a lot to work on. Keeping the family together was our true goal.

I continued to juggle part-time jobs, school, and helping to take care of AJ. We were able with the funds from the lawsuit to upgrade our living arrangement. That was a big help in giving us both something we really wanted and were willing to work on together.

My best buddy in California, John, and a fellow "gamer" helped us move into our new "digs" when Kendyl and I finally were ready to give our marriage and living together as man-and-wife another chance. I hope this "chance" lasts forever!

***

Time seemed to fly by, and AJ was coming up on his third birthday. We needed to start thinking about school for our son. That is definitely Kendyl's forte. She wants to be involved with all of AJ's activities and education. It's also something at which she naturally excels. After what we'd been through, we both needed to feel like we were equals in our partnership as parents, as well as expressing the love between us that needed confidence-boosting too. Thankfully, our love weathered the storm, but we had to learn how to express it through thick-and-thin. Marriage is a challenge every day of the week, every year, every decade. Love is about caring and compromise.

It's a constant learning experience of knowing when to give-and-take, what to let go as trivial, and what to stand your ground on. There's a way of talking to someone to prove your point that doesn't have to be negative. And of course, we both had to be willing to communicate. That's the magic word when it comes to different interests and disagreements. *"Ya'haf'ta' talk about it!"*

As Kendyl put all of her intelligence and confidence into AJ, he became the center of her focus. It was beautiful to watch how her every thought reflected her love for him. It softened me within my soul to see this side of her. How could I ever let go of her? She's my world and the guiding light for our little family. Don't get me wrong, sometimes she can be as overbearing as I am. She ponders excessively over every tiny decision, but I soon realized that her attention to detail is what makes her the ideal partner to get the best of everything for our children.

I had been making my own decisions for so long, it was difficult for me to include someone else in the decision-making process. Maybe Kendyl had felt this way as well when we were first thrown together with an infant to be concerned about. We had to learn how to be part of a team.

At this point in our lives, however, Kendyl's strength in AJ's education and future allowed me to concentrate on my schooling without having to worry about all the overwhelming things that had driven me over the edge when we were apart. All we had really needed was each other, but the grownup version of ourselves who had found their way through trial-by-fire. We had jumped into this with no preparation. We had to acquire it along the way. We had to find out what each of us was good at for the sake of all of us. *"That's what love and marriage is all about!"*

***

"Finishing school was my highest priority. I needed education to provide for my family,

but on a personal level, I also very much needed to accomplish something for myself!"

—Anthony J. Williams, III

There were so many irons in the fire as both Kendyl and I fought to secure our future. Don't let anyone kid you, no matter how much you love a subject, a discipline, a career choice, a "degree," college is hard, constant work, but the knowledge with the confidence that comes from acquiring that knowledge is an experience that will be a deep part of you for the rest of your life.

I was studying online, so I didn't have the distractions that had overwhelmed and ruled me when I first started at the university after Iona Prep High School. I wasn't doing this to party, hook up with a girl, meet people, entertain everyone; I was doing this to make something of myself of which I could be proud, but mostly I was doing this for "us". It wasn't just about me anymore. It was about "MY" family: the wonderful woman who had fallen in love with me and *"oops baby"* that had brought us together. Maybe that's why it finally worked!

My family in New York had shown me the ropes, which I'd almost hung myself with, but once I was thinking clearly again, I could see how my parents' values were engrained in me like something solid etched in stone. Kendyl had the same ideals. We were meant to be together. It was a long, winding road, which of course, we're still very much on.

While still attending school, I started a business venture with John, the dear friend who helped us move and, believe it or not, Leigh, my boss from the repo job, which didn't last very long, but was my first job after rehab. As people say, *"we had history"*. Maybe not the best history, but a connection just the same. My dad always helped his friends out. I watched it happen all the time during my formative years. Thank goodness, I was starting to remember the good things.

This all came together during a particularly rugged time in my education. It was when I had just transitioned to a whole new set of classes. It was grueling and hard as I struggled to learn another system with no comfort zone. All while trying to put together a fledging business from the ground-up. And experience? I didn't have any of that! Leigh had some, of course, and John was young and enthusiastic, just like me, but short on credentials.

I can't tell you how much midnight oil I burned during this phase of my life. We would talk long into the night, split up assignments for the next day or next week, and then go our own way. Some things got done; others didn't. And believe me, it wasn't always me who left the other guys hanging. We all had our share of successes and failures. This business venture, while not making it to the Fortune 500 list, did teach John and me a lot about business. The world was changing so much then with the Internet, online promo, and real-time, video communication.

I was on the brink of the entrepreneur mentality, where anybody with a unique idea and the blood, sweat, tears, gumption, and fortitude to withstand the pressure could make something of themselves—"re-invent themselves"—which is the term I used at the lowest ebb in my existence when I was rushed off to a plane with a strange man to try and save me from myself. Maybe that's why all of this has resonated so much with me. I took the very worst of me, my past, and turned it into something positive. It's my saving grace, and the only way I can live with myself.

These lessons are invaluable skills that I'm still using every day. I used them while I was writing the first draft of this book. I wouldn't let myself sleep at night until I had accomplished something in pouring out my heart through a keyboard and a brightly lit screen in a darkened room. I had to see it to believe that I was actually coming to grips with all that had happened to me. As I've written before, that's how this started. It wasn't until after it was done that I realized maybe, just maybe, someone else was out there suffering to release the past as much as I was. Maybe there are a lot of "somebodies" who needed help like I did.

"Needed help 'like I did'? No, needed help like I do! I will never outlive my past.

It will always be a part of me. It will always make me shudder even when I think it's gone.

It will always come back to haunt me as I admit my weaknesses and failures."

Chapter Forty-nine: Graduation; Career, *"A final solution? I wish!"*

"It felt like the walls were closing in on me! Had all my work to recover been a waste of time? Marriage in and of itself is difficult. Add a baby, sobriety, addiction, finances, a new career?

I felt suffocated! Kendyl was one wall; then parenthood; life and career were the other two—

it was like I was a caged animal, looking for a way out of the box I was stuck in!"

—Anthony J. Williams, III

I was stuck because I wasn't continuing to grow. Who had time for such development? I was merely reacting, putting out fires. I began to think that marriage was an impossible task, especially with two strong-willed people wanting success and *"happily ever after"* at any cost! The cost was a price that might be too much to bear. What would happen then? If we didn't make it? What about AJ? What about having a marriage like my parents, which is all I have ever wanted and dreamed about? *"Why was our relationship and love just too much for me? It was my fault!"*

The emotional roller coaster that Kendyl and I had been on for so long was taking a toll on us. The only thing I felt good about was graduating with my degree, completing a 4-year program in only 3 years, but I was worried that the turbulence we were going through as a family was not just affecting me and Kendyl, but AJ as well. He was getting old enough to feel the vibes in our home, and they weren't good. Everything we did; everything we cared about; everything had to be about our children. It was the only way we could both keep our sanity but having a second child was bringing only heartbreak. Many things were changing but stagnant too! I couldn't keep up!

Kendyl was going through some really hard times. Her keeping her job was crucial because it provided AJ with free schooling, and we needed the health benefits. She suffered in silence after multiple miscarriages. I didn't know what to say to her. I tried, but the right words just wouldn't come; if such a thing as saying the right thing at a time like that is even possible.

We tried marriage counseling again. We had to get some help, but since our first attempt at couples' therapy hadn't really worked for us, I was terrified I was going to lose that which was supposed to give my life meaning. So, we kept asking ourselves, individually without consulting each other, who could we turn to for answers and when had the communication stopped? I don't know why we found it so hard to tell each other what we were thinking and feeling; it just was!

We eventually found Andy and Nancy. They were a blessing and a curse because they were able to define the issues that we had separately brought into the relationship from the very beginning, but never talked about. They were able to give us ideas and tools to fix some of the problems and misunderstandings. They were telling us to have faith in each other, but "faith" without hard work and determination isn't enough. We began to question if "love" was enough?

While going through the process, we found out that Kendyl was pregnant again. It was bittersweet. The fear of losing another baby was almost too much for us to handle. Why was this happening? She'd had no problem with AJ. Was I putting this pressure on her by being in school? At a time like this, your head fills with terrible thoughts: *"Is God punishing me or us for all the mistakes we'd made with addiction and excessive alcohol use?"* Things come back to haunt you that don't really make sense, but you can't deny the hold your past has on you when you look at the same face in the mirror every day. *"I look exactly the same, so maybe I am the same?"*

Had we really changed enough? We would both be recovering addicts for the rest of our lives. Did Kendyl worry that she had somehow hurt her body through addiction? Was she blaming herself, just as I was blaming myself? I think we were both preparing for the worse. We were both in a tailspin with no end to our misery.

AJ, as always, was the only right thing we had ever achieved together. Our baby our child, was a big part of our saving grace.

If I can offer a little bit of advice here, I guess I'd have to say to someone going through this nightmare, this doubt and fear, *"Stop trying to control the outcome and just go with the flow."* There are so many things in life that we just can't anticipate or arrange or change or understand. Why had we lost a brother or sister for AJ? *"There are no answers to why questions."*

I had to accept the pain that Kendyl was going through. No matter how heavy the loss was for me, it was twice as heavy for her. Women are strong, and they can endure so much, but this was the one thing that I ever experienced with the woman I love that I couldn't do anything about; nor could I feel all that she was feeling. Accepting this was sad and made me feel so useless, but it all came back to acceptance, just like in the 12-step program. I had to accept her pain, and she had to weather that pain the only way she knew how … she just couldn't talk about it.

"Kendyl and I had to accept the bad and the good, be there for each other, and understand that in a marriage not all things are equal. Like life, give-and-take isn't always fair."

—Anthony J. Williams, III, and Mrs. Kendyl Williams

Chapter 50: Rainbows or Dark Clouds, *"Will we ever know why?"*

"Both of us were adhering to old patterns: *the blame, shame, and keeping score game.*"

There was one small window of time when we became synchronized; *how do we keep it going?*

Now, we were at the point of talking divorce, but we both knew we still loved each other."

—Anthony J. Williams, III

The new company with my friend John folded right before I got my degree. When he moved to Vegas, I was devastated without him, but I had so much to think about and prepare for with new skills and career dreams. Now was the time for my hard work to begin, but I knew from experience that every positive action has a negative and equal reaction. We needed to join forces to accept my career move and the baby on the way. Both of us were scared of the added strain a baby would bring into our tentative truce. AJ was on his own in many ways, not an infant anymore.

I had won awards with my degree that really perked me up momentarily: Team Building, Leadership, and surprisingly, the Academic Achievement Award. It was sad I couldn't apply these same skills to my fixing my home life. The awards for having a good marriage and a loving family are strictly internal, like overcoming addiction. Somehow you just can't put into words what it really means until you're tested yet again in another area of your life. Recovery is forever because as things change and rearrange, resolve and evolve, the hunger for a fix or a drink sneaks back in.

Every pregnancy is different, and this certainly was prven to us. Kendyl was really sick, so much more so than with AJ, in the early months of her pregnancy All of her symptoms were exaggerated. It didn't seem like she was the same woman who had sheltered and nurtured our child from within just a few years earlier Kendyl's "mom's" intuition crept in without her really knowing it. She didn't share her feelings with me because she was nauseous and tired and worn out. That's enough to depress anyone so they fear the worst. At least, that was what she thought

We saw the same doctor as before. He knew us and we had such a grea relationship with him. After a few months when we were heading to the doctor' office for a checkup on mother and baby's health, we were starting to feel th excitement of being new parents. This was a small window of joy for us to hol onto as things started to alter and shift, becoming confusing. We could feel the light-hearted mood in the room being swallowed up by something bigger than ourselves. The doctor was running additional tests and tensions were running high. Finally, we were told that the baby wasn't going to make it.

Kendyl's face is what I remember most. The look of horror and helplessness etched into her eyes and when the tears finally came it felt like the end of my world. What could I do to make this better? *Nothing could make it better! I tried to make a joke, which really fell flat like the love in my heart. I was nervous and forlorn, but it was Kendyl's body that was involved, not mine.*

This was the first miscarriage, but there would be more. We had so many questions that didn't seem to have any real answers. Another obstacle had invaded our lives that we didn't know how to deal with, and there are no courses in overcoming death before life begins. You can't understand the magnitude of this until you experience it as a couple, as a union. I wouldn't wish this loss and emptiness on anyone, but yet we knew miscarriages happened to good people like us.

Moving past this failure and this feeling that we did something wrong was hard enough, but watching this happen to the woman you love and the mother of your beautiful son, now a strong, scrapping toddler was complicated, and there are really no words to express the emptiness.

The absoluteness of an ending that never really had a beginning changes the way you view things, especially your strong and everlasting faith in the divine. Each child is a gift from God. That was how we both had been raised. The physical and mental anguish a woman goes through with this, knowing the baby is already "gone" inside her. I just shake my head as I sit here and write this. It always brings tears creeping down my face, that I never let Kendyl see.

Our problems with our marriage and jobs and money and everything else paled in comparison. We started talking to each other that day, and it probably saved our love, our marriage, and our family. But what a price to pay!

Chapter Fifty-one: Nightmare on the 15, *"Our little girl? Yeah!"*

The best way for me to tell you about this blessed event is in-person; at least that's what people, mostly my friends, tell me. I am very animated in the telling, and my excitement is palpable. I'll do the best I can using the written words on this page.

There is six years between AJ and our daughter, Italia. It was such a difficult pregnancy with the constant fear of miscarriage and trying to talk our way through all the other issues. The day we found out it was a little girl was exciting but confusing too. This was like starting all over again from scratch. We were both nervous wrecks. The care, clothes, toys, everything was going to be different. Were we prepared? Six years is a long time. You forget what it's like. You remember the exhaustion and lack of sleep, but there was AJ to think of as well.

My little Bubby ... AJ took the news of having a sister really well. He was going to be a big brother, but it wasn't quite real to him. He was more concerned with toys and television shows and what was for dinner. But as the pregnancy progressed, even though each checkup was terrifying for us as parents, we started to get excited about it. The fear did lessen, somewhat.

December 5, 2017 was the due date that was given to Kendyl by the doctors. On that day, she had an appointment. He decided to perform a procedure which would induce labor. I didn't even know about it until after it was over. In my mind, I marveled at the idea—the human body is an incredible creation—*"Hmm...so the doctor can just scrape her vagina and make things happen? But why were we going home instead of straight to the hospital?"* I was totally in the dark.

Kendyl had a complete birthing plan with this pregnancy: hospital, doctors, some preparatory items like cloth diapers and such at home. Procedures and familiar medical roles had changed a lot in past six years as well. It was a natural birth plan, which includes a *doula,* a woman to advise the mother through ... well, through all of it.

At 11:30 p.m. that night, we were still waiting at home. I finished up some loose ends connected to work because I was going to be a little busy the next few days, right? I headed upstairs to bed after my normal security routine. I checked on AJ. He was asleep. This kid sleeps solid! He gets the covers all twisted up and scrunched up in odd directions, but Kendyl had kept him on a sleep schedule since he was 3 months old. That was a big help. I straightened things out and tucked him back in. He woke up slightly but went right back to sleep before I even left the room.

When I went in the make-shift bedroom downstairs, Kendyl looked like she was starting to have some pain. I went through my regular, nightly routine which includes taking my heart meds, and before our kiss good night, I asked her, "Kendyl, you going to have this baby very soon?"

"No," she replied. "Not anytime soon, I don't think." Just as the words came out of her mouth, she winced in pain.

"Let's go to the hospital," I insisted. We went back-and-forth on that for a few minutes.

It was going to be a long night. I remembered the false alarm we had with AJ. I was getting ready to take a shower, so I'd be ready. I was going into survival mode. Can't have the baby on the floor at home! Kendyl was texting with the doula, who was trying to assess what stage she was in. The doula suggested that I try to get some sleep. If we got there too early, they wouldn't admit her, and the hospital was 45 minutes away.

Every pregnancy and every birth are so totally different. Kendyl needed injections in her back with AJ. There's no magical formula to foresee what is to come. Maybe Kendyl didn't know what level of pain she was in because the shots with AJ covered up some of the pain, but that was hindsight on my part. She knew it would be worse this time initially. So did the doula. In fact, they texted all night, which I didn't know then. Why didn't she come over? I'm still upset over that!

It was AJ who woke me up at 5:30 a.m. in the morning, December 6th. He said, "Mommy hurts, and she can't walk up the stairs to get you." I was awake in an instant, "*TIME TO MOVE!*" I got dressed, brushed my teeth, grabbed the phone. The car was already packed from the night before. Simple, right? Just get to the hospital. Only Kendyl had been in labor all night! Where was the doula? I'm really upset by now. I call her on Kendyl's phone. She got there 15 minutes later. We had to wait for her just to tell us that Kendyl needed to go to the hospital. *"No, shit, lady!"*

I get AJ in the car, pull it out of the garage; the doula helps Kendyl to the car. I can see and feel the pain, just like it's my own. I swear to you, I felt it! I couldn't look at her and not feel it.

I race down local streets to get to the 15 freeway. All I could think about was driving faster to get to the hospital in time. My mother-in-law is on the phone at this point, asking us to meet her at the off-ramp to her home. I think I was rude but I tell her to meet us at the hospital. I didn't have time to tell her how serious this was before I ended the call. Had to keep my eyes on the road!

I passed Rainbow Road on 15 South. *Traffic is backing up! A sea of taillights!* I didn't know what to do, but then I just kept going on the shoulder. Dangerous, yes, but…? My pregnant wife and 6-year old son are in the car. I put on my hazard lights. I was hoping a cop would pull me over so I could get help!

I knew what labor sounded like. I was there when AJ was born. The sounds from the front seat were definitely not human. AJ from the backseat says he's bored. He wants the radio on. "Bubby, we need to be a team to help Mommy. We need to work together, okay?" Anyway, he pulled out a drawing pad from his stuff and kept busy.

We went about 2 miles on the shoulder, and I got back on the freeway. I began to get a sick feeling in the pit of my stomach that we weren't going to make it to the hospital. Maybe, we would. I'm driving like a maniac, trying to get pulled over on the freeway … anything to get some help! I was panicking, sweating bullets. I was silent, though; I couldn't upset Kendyl and AJ. I wasn't screaming or freaking. I had to keep it together. My guts were in my throat! I just kept driving. Then I see a sheriff's vehicle in the far-left lane. I tell them both to hang on as I tried to get through traffic to the officer. I wasn't thinking anything through. I just needed help!

Kendyl, God what a woman! My eyes fill with tears now just thinking about it, reliving it all again. It happens every time I think of it. She's grunting in pain, out just like an actress in a movie, she tells me, "Please, be careful." And the leading man says, "Don't worry, baby; this is the one thing I'm good at." Now I'm a stunt driver, and I get to say one cheesy line to make me feel good. I was just reacting. Sheer adrenaline. AJ is in the backseat; Kendyl in the front with me.

I pull up to the sheriff, hanging half out of the car yelling, "Pomerado! She's in labor! We need help!" AJ is finally interested in the goings on; he sees the cop and realizes we're traveling fast! The look on the cop's face is one of utter and complete shock. He can see Kendyl. As long as I live, I will never forget the look on his face. He's just driving to work, like everybody else. He taps his brakes, lines up behind us, puts his lights on, and waves at me to GO! I'm still trying to get to the hospital. I gun it and pray. Then he pulls up beside us. "You're not going to make it," he yells across at me. At this point, I had to agree. The traffic, morning rush-hour. He yells to me that he's contacted an ambulance and firetruck. We need to get off the freeway quickly. Then, I glanced in the rearview mirror and was instantly sobered … an exit, Gopher Canyon Road. Due to the cop, we had about 200 feet of clearance behind the car. I called the doula, let her know the ramp and exit, called my mother-in-law too. I honestly have no idea how I managed this. I cut the wheel hard to the right; the cop is following me; the doula says she's only a minute or two out. But even that was too long. Now I had to focus on delivering our baby.

I pull off the exit, open all the doors to the car. Pull AJ from the backseat. The officer grabs AJ so he doesn't wander into the traffic. It all happened so fast. The doula is there with Kendyl. It was only a matter of seconds, but it felt like an eternity. The baby is in my wife's yoga pants. The doula helps me get the baby and places her on Kendyl's stomach. I'm in bona fide, medical shock, shaking like a leaf and freezing cold ... yeah, in San Diego!

I start yelling, "The Cord! The Cord!" It's wrapped around the baby, tangled up from the yoga pants. The doula fixes the cord and tells me the baby is breathing. I can't believe it! She's okay! Kendyl is okay, I think?

The ambulance and the firetruck show up ... like 30-45 seconds after we pulled over, but it felt so much longer. It felt like 10-15 minutes. I get loud again and ask someone to cover the baby. Someone asks me if I want to cut the cord. I reply, "Yes, I'll cut the cord, but someone needs to cover this f***ing baby!" The crew, they were young guys. They didn't know much more than I did. Only one of the guys actually helped with the birth. We get Kendyl and the baby in the ambulance. They're both breathing. They're off to the hospital.

I stayed where I was. I mean, AJ and the car. What a mess! Who would clean it up? It looked like someone had murdered a moose in the front seat. The only thing that really registered was AJ's expression at seeing his mom and new sister in the front seat after the birth. He was fine. He was curious. He wanted to meet his sister. Yeah, I walked him up to car before the paramedics transferred them to the ambulance. "Ewe, there's poop!" AJ says, and then "What is that?" I saw my mother-in-law's car. I hurried him over, and she took him home with her.

I grabbed a few towels, tried to clean some of it. The firefighter crew handed me napkins and wipes to help with cleaning the front seat. The officer asked me if I was okay. I responded honestly, "No, I'm not." Somehow, we pulled the mats out of the car, covered them with dirt to dry them out. It worked. We put them in the trunk. The car was now cleaner than it had been.

I wasn't prepared for any of this. *Who could be?* The memory, however, is with me every time I look at Kendyl and at "our little girl".

Chapter Fifty-two: The Aftermath, *"How do I describe it? I can't!"*

The shock was overwhelming after the ambulance left with Kendyl and Italia. AJ was already with his grandmother getting into her car headed to their house, which had been part of the original plan. The first time the officer asked, "Are you okay?" I wasn't; it was a hard *"no"*. I mentally blacked out immediately after knowing everyone was safe. I was just trying to keep it together once reality set in, and I faced the reality that the car was a mess.

The officer cautiously approached me for a second time. He was slowly moving towards me, asking the million-dollar question, "Are you okay?" Face flushed bright red, brains still scrambled, and the response was mildly put, "I'll be okay." The shock was one thing, but the realization of having to clean this car was another. The whole situation was intense with this car as clean as it was going to get with the help of the firefighters. My mind was as clear as it was going to be; it was time to move.

In the car, windows rolled down and the music turned up, still had me feeling uneasy on my way to the hospital. I couldn't shake the thought of the baby exposed to the cold for too long. It didn't matter now; the only priority was making it to the hospital in one piece. I parked the car and began sprinting into the hospital.

My heart found its way into my throat as I entered the room only to see Italia hooked up to a heater. My eyes were laser-focused on my *"little girl."* She was so cold, and here came the feelings of helplessness again.

Kendyl was in the bathroom getting cleaned up with the help of a nurse. I knew she was going to be fine as she was up and about the moment she arrived at the hospital. It was such a relief at an important moment. We needed each other.

Still unable to fully process the events of today, there were other things that needed our attention. Italia must have known I was there holding her hand as her body fought to bring her temperature back to stable levels. She let my hand go once her temperature was at a safe level.

The doula was in the room, taking pictures of everyone. My anxiety was growing, just thinking of the car smelling like a burnt barn. I laid out this plan. The doula and I got into our cars and headed to the detail shop near my house. I jumped out of my car and tossed the attendant the keys. I had already spoken with the owner on the phone and told him the whole story. They knew my interaction would be brief. It was time to get back to my house, pick up our other car, and head back to the hospital.

Alone, confused, and in desperate need of a mental vacation, it took about 30 minutes for me to compose myself before heading back to the hospital. Notifications began to alert my phone about the fires in the area. It never registered how close we were to the fires. Little did we know that as Italia was being born, we were dangerously close to the fires raging on the other side of the hill. I received a text from Kendyl letting me know the hospital shared our concern about the fires, and the freeway might get shut down temporarily. It was time to move while I still could.

As I was driving down the freeway, the anxiety and fear began to build. The entire morning began replaying in my head with each mile I drove. A snap judgment landed me at the scene of the birth. I felt the need to gather a memento. Grabbing a paper bag and placing some dirt and a few flowers from the scene into it seemed like a refreshing reminder. It was the best I could do with what I had at the moment.

This entire day was a blur as time seemed to stop multiple times. Pulling back up to the hospital didn't calm any nerves; I was a wreck. I couldn't help but be afraid, but I knew this was a healthy fear. I accepted my powerlessness along with the thought that life was going to get significantly more complicated. All the tests completed and in minutes, our little girl would be our responsibility.

The doctors and nurses came back into the room with pamphlets in hand. Our baby had a tongue tie and a lip tie, top and bottom. There was little doubt that this would complicate breastfeeding and speech if not attended to in a timely fashion. My brain couldn't help but go immediately go to my childhood and the disabilities I faced. My heart sank, thinking she would struggle with a speech impediment. In the end, this is not a significant cause for worry, but if you have been following along this whole time, I'm sure you would share the same concern.

The upcoming months would be exhausting. Italia had trouble latching during breastfeeding causing gas to force her to toss and turn throughout her naps. It didn't help the gas made it sound like she was gurgling while she was sleeping. AJ loves his sister, but he's always begging for attention. The gap in age was leaving us overreached and hanging on by a thread.

"Despite the ups and downs, somehow, we made it. I lost both of my jobs right around Italia's first birthday. Out of work for seven months, completely draining our savings to stay alive. Times haven't been the best, and regardless of the circumstances I'm still here.

We are still here."

—Anthony J. Williams, III

Epilogue & Additional Information

Everything that has been written up to this very word is with the hope you, my reader, will draw strength in knowing you are not alone. My story is unique to me as yours is unique to you. I was brave enough to explore, hoping you would do the same. I'm still standing because of the love and support afforded to me. There were plenty of times giving up seemed the only option. It always feels that way, and with every misstep or misfortune, fear strikes, leaving your stomach in knots. Left unchecked, it poisons your mind, having you believe you are worthless. Finding a way out is the only hope. It's a lie. Life is beautiful.

This book helped heal my soul. I'm nowhere near perfect or comfortable with every aspect of my life. I accept it, and that's the difference. The thoughts of my past could cripple me if I let them. I can't give them that power, and I won't let those life events, some of which were my own fault, define me. It's just an experience, all of this was a bunch of lessons to show you no matter what, you can make it through. Nothing lasts forever; we all adapt, reinvent, fear, and accept the next experience which will help us grow. Forgive yourself, love yourself, accept yourself, and the world will be better for it.

This book was not created to be a life-hack or a walkthrough to give someone else advice, guiding you every step of the way. It was for my own personal healing. We need to get away from the instant gratification and the expectation that the answer is right there, and we need it now! That's not the case for many. It most likely is not the case for you. One thing that helped me through everything was knowing I am not alone. The living examples of molestation, addiction, disease, surgery, inadequacy, pain, fear, hate, and love are here as a guide that someone else made it through. It's that simple; it's hope.

Whatever my purpose, at least I'll be there to succeed or fail. In failure, there are lessons in which we can grow, and in success, there are lessons we can be proud of and prepare for others. It may not be evident now, but you will know when the time comes to suit up and show up. Giving your best is all you can do, keeping the perspective you don't control the outcome. Life slowly gets a little easier if you work at it.

I have been through emotional hell, and some could make the argument physical as well. I hope that helps someone else. I hope the pain I endured helps someone get through it quickly as we can never avoid pain. We need tools in our toolbox, and this book is a tool. It's a powerful tool, and that's why I decided to expose myself. All that pain needed to be directed somewhere to avoid utter destruction. If you still feel this way, reread it, and know there is no one answer to solve your problems. It is hard to be vulnerable, but that doesn't mean you can't be. You must if you truly want to grow.

We can do more as a society to help those in need. We, the people, can do it without the bluster of Hollywood or political circles. There is some good work being done to help those in need. I ask only one thing; can we please base our want and need to improve on attraction rather than promotion? These get confused very quickly, along with their intentions.

Scandals, inappropriate behavior, and divisiveness diverted me from reaching out to politicians and Hollywood figures. Their polarized views to benefit themselves, and their circles never have the masses in mind. We are taught to hate or disagree with each other leaving us divided from birth. Our children learn how to navigate political speech before determining what our differences indeed are, in contrast to their own.

Let's work together while working for each other. We can do that. It's what has made us the civilization we are today. Let's tell stories truthfully, engage lovingly, and be vulnerable. It's the only way we can heal. I did all of this for you. Thank you for helping me!

***

As each page turns another scar is torn open. The only way to heal is speaking about the pain. This journey was meant to be a rollercoaster. Events in my life leave a pit in my stomach as most have no immediate solution. The mind is a funny thing. Its ability to create an alternate reality or ego allows you to survive some of the most insufferable events.

I'll never be able to say, "I know how you feel", but I can definitely relate. No one can ever feel your pain; it's yours. My story was not made to point fingers with the expectations of a parade or celebration. Despite there being a time when the expectations were exactly that. I honestly do not know what most people think of me, and that's why I do not care because I know I cannot control what others think. I learned that from experiencing so much pain from wanting acceptance. I never felt right, always felt different, and it didn't matter; I wasn't happy with me. I thought everything was my own fault, and some of it was; yet, some it wasn't. It's just what life throws at you while you grow and evolve based on the decisions you make.

I am forever grateful to my family, friends, colleagues, and acquaintances for all of the support they have provided long before this book was ever written. All of my experiences have opened me up to thinking, "What kind of world will this be for my kids and their kids?" The pain they feel today is real, and we must support their mistakes as much as their accomplishments. This world today reminds me of a period of my life where I felt the most pain. The need to be perfect with the inability to be perfect.

Graduating from college was a huge accomplishment for me. Despite all the turbulence my wife and I both experienced during these times, it was not lost on us that both of us were affected. It's inevitable that the child would feel some of it as well. It's always about the children, and when looking back through an objective lens, the only way to navigate it without giving up is to make it all about the kids.

Marriage, in and of itself, is difficult; it's almost an impossible task especially with two people wanting success at any cost. The cost is a variable that comes at a price for some that is too costly to bare. The emotional roller coaster takes its toll when two individuals are trying to get their lives together, then add a child into the mix. It's an unexplored territory, and the only way to navigate this is to learn each day by gaining experience minute-by-minute.

Marriage counseling is what saved a broken attempt at trying to correct it ourselves. We had no chance at fixing the broken pieces without some help. The question we kept asking ourselves was who could help? We eventually found that help in Andy and Nancy. It was a blessing and a curse because now we knew the issues we carried into this relationship with no tools with which to fix any of it. We are now gaining those tools, but like everything else it's up to us to use those tools. Faith without work is death. There is no movement in death; we both learned this from an early age, but now it is ever present in our lives.

Raising a son is one of the best accomplishments in my life. I know Kendyl feels the same as she has been a phenomenal mother. She endured pain I could never know anything about. When we experienced failed pregnancies that wasn't something that I could just go put my hand on her back and say, "It's going to be okay". Yet, it never feels like it will be okay. Nothing can prepare a person for losing a child even if you never met them. We were blessed in a sense to have a failed pregnancy rather than to have the child be born only to lose them instantly. We experienced two of those, and that was enough for me to say, "I'm done with trying." Thinking about it further we were never actually trying, but it was something that was part of our lives, leaving little scars along the way and softening the hardened shell for what was to come.

When finding out we were about to have another baby, it was bittersweet. The fear of losing another child was almost too much to handle. Your head fills with terrible thoughts and any little adjustment needed only forces you to prepare for the worst. It's a terrible way to live and a terrible way to approach bringing a child into the world. If I were to give any advice it would be this, "Stop trying to control the outcome and just go with the flow." Easier said than done, but we must keep in mind that for the ones not carrying the baby we will never know the toll it takes on the mental and physical aspects of the woman. On the other hand, men need to understand it is a heavier burden to bear than they could ever imagine. No matter how heavy, it is never as heavy as the responsibility the woman endures.

This past year:

This past year has been a hell of a ride! I didn't quit everything I love to do to write this book. In fact, I intentionally didn't quit everything because I knew the difficulty that comes with the process. This was a selfish inquiry that blossomed into something far greater than ever intended. Italia being born forced many changes in our home. Accustomed to AJ having a sleep schedule and finally being able to exert his own individuality was short lived. Italia being born would only reset everything back 6.5 years. You never forget being a parent but having a six-and-a-half-year gap between kids means you need to brush up on some skills. Sleep deprivation is one of the major aspects of having a new baby for which parents will never become accustomed.

The amount of support for each other and our family that took place this last year is unreal. Like most people I have amazing support but as a person who doesn't reach out and ask for it regularly, it's sometimes flees from my memory like a thought in the wind. The job I thought would take my career to the next level folded. Despite the boss being an asshole who made poor decisions before I ever entered the doors, the majority of people there knew what he was for exactly what he is, a con. My parents came to visit for Thanksgiving and the day after they arrived, I got the news the job was done. I already had a second job with the sole intent of paying off debt especially since Italia was going to be turning one year old in a few weeks.

A month after the second job folded too, however, it was on to the races to find work. My buddy Keith would chat with me via text as I checked on his mental health as well as my own. The pressure was mounting, and the funds were running lower each month.

The clock was ticking, and the options were fleeting due to the level of experience I had gained over the years. I had many skills but did not consider myself a certified expert in one specific thing. Anyone who has been job searching will understand completely. The jobs are plentiful if you have the right networks. Networking is still the primary source of finding a job and proved to be correct as it is the exact way that I landed my current position. I had too much experience but not enough in some areas to be considered for some high-profile positions. I was bitter at first but as it always does, it worked out in the end. I was a few weeks away from pulling the plug on any ventures in California. My next step was going to be living with family back in New York to try to get back on our feet again. I'm grateful there is not an issue in returning to my family.

I continue to try and make sure I'm around long enough for my kids to have a father. This doesn't discount the damage I have done to my body over the years. I am fully aware of my actions and try every day to be a better person. I'm amazed this story got finished. Opening all of those wounds at the same time hurt me all over again but was well worth it if someone else finds a sliver of hope in my message. I'm still in pain knowing time is precious, knowing not everyone is given the opportunity to experience life to its fullest. I can say in all sincerity that I have, and my heart is happy.

The pain of being touched at a young age will never go away, but it no longer haunts or controls me. Failing to follow my dream is part of who I am as is all the pain and pleasures of my life. Close calls with death and self-destruction only hardened my soul. It took writing this to soften it up. Marriage and the birth of my kids changed me as a man. Ultimately, I am human.

It took me a very long time to truly feel what you are about to read in conclusion to my story. I want everyone who reads this to understand the change and growth that has taken place. My self-awareness is what has allowed me to survive through all of this turmoil, uncertainty, and self-doubt. I have written a little something for a few of the most important people in my life.

To my son AJ:

You are all I ever wanted once hearing the news I was to be a father. There was a part of me that felt relief like somehow, I would be given a redo in my life. I could live vicariously through you, and all would be forgotten. Yet, the pain never subsided, and the realization quickly hit me that if I kept this way of thinking I would never truly enjoy who you are and who you would grow up to become.

Every time I look at you, it is immediate; I love you more than life itself. I'm tough on you because I want you to succeed, be adaptable, and understand this can be an ugly world. If I know anything it is that no matter how tough I am on you, there is no question in either of our minds; I have your back. I will never leave that position whether I am here in skin or spirit. Thank you for teaching me what it is to be a man. I love you, *"Bubby"*.

To my wife Kendyl:

There are many times I wonder why and how you are still here? I know the answers now, but it took a long time to understand this is what a family is all about. Thank you for showing me that. Your question, "Who's going to tell you besides me?", rings clear in my head on a daily basis. You stepped up when others stepped away. You stepped up despite all of your insecurities, and our children are amazing because of it. Time has been and always will be your biggest request. I understand that now. Despite all of the ups and downs you were there, and I will forever be in debt to you for that. "I love you" just isn't strong enough. My words cannot match the strength you have exhibited as a mother, wife, and friend. Whenever, wherever I am there. Thank you for helping to shape me into the man I am today. We do love each other.

To my daughter Italia:

AJ is absolutely a hard act to follow. I never knew my heart had more room to love another. You changed that the second I laid eyes on you. Your induction into this world shocked everyone, and in hindsight, it was perfectly fitting for you. You softened me in ways I never knew possible, changing me forever. As with AJ, my role is to protect and guide you through a world that can be unforgiving and ugly. I intend to provide you with all the tools necessary to succeed including love. We speak often without words, and one look from you can wipe away the worst feelings on the worst days. You alone hold a key to my heart. When you are old enough to read this, and I hope that you do, just know I love you more each day. Thank you for bringing light into a dark place of my heart. I love you *"Little girl."*

***

I have thanked my family and supporters throughout this book and firmly believe the feeling is mutual and reciprocated. I am grateful knowing my awareness has grown due to the influences in my life. The one thing that saved me through everything was love and relationships. I hope we can get back to that!

Anthony J. Williams, III

FEEL FREE TO CONNECT:

Facebook: https://www.facebook.com/OnBorrowedTimeAuthor

LinkedIn: https://www.linkedin.com/company/on-borrowed-time-the-reinvention-of-a-lost-soul

Twitter: https://twitter.com/borrowed_on

Instagram: https://www.instagram.com/on_borrowed_time_author/